any color so long as it's black...

any color so long as it's black...

the first fifty years of
automobile advertising

Peter Roberts

David & Charles Newton Abbot·London·Vancouver

Mein Benz!!

ISBN 0 7153 7239 4
©Peter Roberts 1976

Set in 11 on 13pt Times Monophoto
by Keyspools Limited,
Golborne, Lancs
and printed by Mondadori, Italy
for David & Charles (Publishers) Limited
Brunel House, Newton Abbot, Devon

Published in Canada
by Douglas David & Charles Limited
1875 Welch Street, North Vancouver, BC

Contents

Introduction

Advertising has been described as a barometer of public taste, but like so many accepted statements, this is only a part-truth. When applied successfully, it can be not only the graph of shifting preferences but the means whereby preferences are made to swing in one direction or another. Conversely it is capable of monumental misjudgment – both of timing and mood – and often is, at most, a distorted reflection of the preferences it seeks to influence.

The advertisements within these pages have largely ceased to serve their original purpose. The public to which they were directed has ceased to exist, the companies and products which they so earnestly promoted have moved on – or passed on – and no longer require to rely upon them. The fashions, conditions and moods which dictated their messages and the manner of their presentation are so much fading history.

Conclusions drawn from source material which was originally designed for an entirely different purpose must be tempered with a discretion born of the knowledge that whilst we have the benefit of hindsight, most of us, by our lack of years, are denied the insight which would enable us to read the contents of this book through the eyes of those for whom it was originally intended. And since the attitudes of those early buyers and copywriters cannot be recreated, any speculation as to the influence of the material upon the public can be no more than conjecture.

We do have one advantage though. In approaching the advertisements without an attitude of *caveat emptor*, since the choice of purchase is no longer open to us, we can enjoy their comments on the manners and mores of a bygone age without prejudice or bias.

And they still can teach us a great deal about the past.

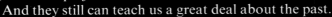

AS SILENT AS ITS SHADOW

The New Market

The pattern of advertising has generally followed the pattern of trade; for centuries it had remained totally unaltered. Such advertising as there was remained purely on a local basis, and the sign displayed outside the Eighteenth Century apothecary's shop announcing his latest cure for the night vapours appealed to exactly the same local audience as had the inscription upon the wall in Pompeii exhorting the citizenry to buy their togas from Claudius Minimus. For the most part, goods were made or grown locally in sufficient quantities to satisfy local demand only, and such commodities as silks and spices which were brought from abroad, were handled initially by merchants on a wholesale basis and thence distributed to large centers of population where, once again, their advertisement would have been of a purely local nature by those retailers who purveyed them.

It was not until the late Eighteenth Century, with the coming of the industrial revolution, that this pattern was interrupted to any great degree. Even then, the baker who knew he could sell only five dozen loaves was a fool if he baked more, and the appetizing smell which issued from his premises was normally the only form of advertisement he needed. With the mechanization of industry, however, the manufacturer was faced with the dilemma of having the ability to produce far more than he could sell within the normal radius of his activity, and at a far cheaper price per item too, whilst at the same time lacking the means of communication by which he could bring his product to the notice of sufficiently wide a clientele to justify the increased output.

In this respect the inland manufacturer suffered a distinct disadvantage, when compared with the merchant based in a coastal port or in a city having direct river access to the sea. For centuries sea trade had been carried on all over the world, and by the late Eighteenth Century had achieved a high level of sophistication. By contrast, communication on land was hampered by a complete lack of good roads and suitable transport, and was beset by the hazards of footpads and highwaymen. It meant that it was considerably simpler to send goods from, say, Britain to France than from one inland city to another.

So far as consumer products such as clothing and hardware were concerned, there were some alleviating factors affecting this dilemma, however, and not least of these was the tendency for larger communities to spring up round the manufacturing centers. The populations of these areas were drawn mainly from the outlying agricultural districts, attracted by the employment opportunities created for unskilled workers, and this movement of population created fresh markets on the manufacturing doorstep. So to some extent some manufacturing was self-propagating, but there was still a growing need for sales outlets further afield.

Whilst the influence of the turnpike roads in Britain assisted communication to an extent, America, which until comparatively recently, was 'simpler to sail round than to travel over' suffered from isolation. And since the availability of natural resources essential to industry tended to be centered in inland areas – Britain's coalfields in the Midlands and the North East, America's coalfields in Pittsburgh, and Germany's Ruhr district, for instance – there became a pressing need for rapid and reliable inland transport. That need was met with the development of the railways in the early Nineteenth Century, and since no single factor has had more lasting influence upon the pattern of trade it is not, perhaps, surprising that advertising on a national – and international – level, and as we know it today, really dates from that time. It would be convenient to say that the change took place overnight, but history unrolls with an irritating

BENZ & CIE

RHEINISCHE GASMOTOREN-FABRIK

Gegründet im Jahre 1883.   **MANNHEIM.**   Gegründet im Jahre 1883.

Patent-Motor-Wagen „Benz"

Patentirt in Deutschland

sowie in allen anderen Industrie-Staaten der Welt.

lack of promptness; traditional overlapping transitional, so that trends can often only be detected after they have already become manifest to all. It is, however, in his ability to detect these minimal stirrings and to interpret them correctly, that the successful advertiser finds himself able to influence a potential market, awaken a latent one, or, on occasions, to create one. It did not take the Nineteenth-Century entrepreneur long to discover this.

With his factory ready to produce his goods, and the railways eager to carry them, it was but a simple step for the manufacturer to stimulate greater demand. This he did by advertisement; in the daily papers (of which there were many, both local and national), in railway carriages and termini, on hoardings and in the guide books of resorts which the railways made accessible to the traveler.

By the time the motor car made its debut, advertising in the form by which we know it today was an accepted part of the scene; it could even be said to have run amok in some cases. If Hudson's Soap had the temerity to use the head of Queen Victoria to publicize their product – *The subject's friend – home and clothes as clean as a rose* – then surely the sky could be the limit. Looking at any scenic illustration taken from the capitals of the world during the 1880's, the dominating sight is advertisement. From every wall, building, horse-bus and carrier's cart, newspaper, guide book, magazine or pamphlet, one was directed or persuaded into what to read, eat, see, drink, wear, travel on, or in, or to, and into treating a hundred-and-one curious ailments with patent medicines.

To the point though it may be, and lacking in imagination, one has to admire the quality of the engraving in this early Benz advertisement.

Benz & Cie**,** Rheinische Gasmotoren-Fabrik, **Mannheim.**

Motor „Velociped."

In diesem Velociped befindet sich eine Maschine von ca. 1½ Pferdekräften.

Preis:

Das Velociped complett mit Laternen . . . . . kostet **Mark 2000.—**

Gewicht des Velocipedes mit Maschine ca. 280 Kilo.

Dimensionen:

Aeusserste Länge des Velocipedes	.	.	.	.	.	2 Meter	25 cm.
„ Breite „	„	.	.	.	.	1 „	25 „
„ Höhe „	„	.	.	.	.	1 „	25 „

Art Nouveau and the Bicycle Poster

In contrast to the vulgar display that ushered in a new, profit-conscious age, the very earliest attempts to persuade a suspicious and reluctant public to abandon the horse for the motor car were models of restraint and taste. But not for long; as soon as it became apparent that a potentially major market existed (and because of restrictive legislation against the motor car, this took a little longer in Britain) the flood-gates opened, and many advertisements for motor cars propounded their claims with more enthusiasm than accuracy.

Whilst, historically speaking, it is generally accepted that the bicycle industry begat the motor car industry (and was itself an outgrowth of the sewing machine boom) both the 'modern' bicycle and the motor car were first built within a dozen years of each other.

The bicycle was a commercial proposition virtually from the word 'go', but the motor car passed through a painfully slow period of gestation and showed

Bicycle art transitional 1899: compared to the motor car, the bicycle lady is animated. She is now, alas, fully clothed and, following Beardsley perhaps, a little sinister.

Der erste Automobilprospekt der OPEL-WERKE aus dem Jahre 1899

Motorwagen

OPEL

ADAM OPEL

Rüsselsheim a. M.

Whilst they were accompanied by a caption which assured prospective buyers that the 1897 Oldsmobile (the first) shown here, was 'practically noiseless and impossible to explode' the occupants look none too relaxed.

Opposite: bicycle art transitional: both bicycle and car are now inanimate, the maiden is no longer 'topless' although still diaphanous, and a 'radiator' badge (*Le Trefle à Quatre*) is displayed. (National Motor Museum)

obvious promise only from the late 'Nineties. By this time bicycle fever was beginning to burn itself out and a number of manufacturers were looking for an alternative line with which to cushion themselves against a possible slump. The motor car provided the answer.

So there were two distinct types of Victorian advertisement – the nuts-and-bolts, and the Art Nouveau. The meticulously executed engravings of the 1888 Benz (page 9) and the slightly later examples from the same factory at Mannheim (pages 10 & 50) echo the simple honesty of the inventor himself, and can be compared more to a patent specification, rather than the eulogies of a sales department. Little or no attempt is made to influence the potential purchaser, the occupants of the vehicle are eminently respectable, and the image created is without romance or imagination. Which is, of course, exactly what the advertising catalogues of which they are part, were intended to convey. Whilst slightly less restrained, the Daimler announcement (right) projects the same somewhat monochrome theme, and stresses the serious vein in which the customer is approached. Not so, however, the 1897 version (page 14) which is refreshing for the period.

The bicycle boom coincided with the 'naughty' 'Nineties, an era synonymous with the Follies, the Moulin Rouge, the 'decadent' art of Aubrey Beardsley – and the golden age of the French poster. Lithographic art had reached a zenith by this time, with artists of the calibre of Lautrec and Jules Cheret capturing exactly the mood of the period. The bicycle industry 'adopted' the art poster and elevated it to a position in the art world which has scarcely been equalled by any advertising medium since. Employing much of the technique normally associated with 'art nouveau', the classic bicycle poster shared with this art form the adulation of the female form – of which not much had been seen for some time. Following hard upon the heels of a period noted for its stuffy moral code, there was something very refreshing in the manner of presentation, and only the bigot could take offence at the innocently nubile maidens depicted.

Photography, a comparatively new toy, had also become the rage and it was not long before manufacturers began to make increasing use of the photographer's, rather than the artist's, studio to promote their wares. Allied to contemporary type-faces the marriage was not always happy aesthetically, and whilst it may have eliminated any tendency towards artist's licence in the

Stolid Teuton, and no hint of humour here. Daimler *circa* 1890.

Pennington said it, but Daimler said it better in 1897:

'A Daimler is a handy beast
It draws like an ox – you can see it here –
It doesn't eat when in the stall
And only drinks when work's done.
It also does your threshing, sawing and pumping
When money's short, as often happens,
It can't catch foot and mouth disease,
And plays no wicked tricks on you.
It won't toss you on its horn in anger,
Nor eat up your good corn,
So buy yourself a beast like this
And be equipped for good and all.'

The Duryea may have been 'a carriage, not a machine', but there is nothing poetic about this unhappy marriage between photography and assorted typefaces, in 1897. Two years later, the Fiat effort (*Right*) is almost as bad.

illustration, this was often more than compensated for in the flowery and ambiguous prose with which the somewhat blotchy photos were accompanied (above and opposite).

The Profiteers

America, possibly because of her 'wild colonial boy' image, has always been popularly credited with being the spiritual home of the 'pushy' hard-sell salesman. The conception which, until relatively recently, readily sprung to the average non-American mind would have fallen into one of two distinct categories; the cigar smoking, astrakhan-collared share pusher from Wall Street, and the rainmaker, potion pedalling, traveling 'Doctor'. Disconcerting though it may be to those who delight in exploding popular myths, the two men who played perhaps the largest part in advertising (if not advancing) the motor car in America, fell exactly into these archetypal moulds.

The first was self-styled 'Professor' W. W. Austen, who made a good living exhibiting (and sometimes claiming to be the inventor of) the steam buggies and velocipedes built by Sylvestor Roper in Roxbury, Massachusetts. He gave demonstrations at County Fairs and circuses all over the country from the 1860's onward and eventually met a sticky end when he collided with another steamer at the Charles River cycle track in Boston in 1895.

The other, and unfortunately more influential of the two, was Edward Joel Pennington, born in Franklin Township, Indiana, in 1858. He was one of those rare individuals who combined the talents of technical invention, vision and salesmanship. He was also a crook. Any man who could, however, convince a sceptical public that his vehicles were capable of jumping a sixty-five feet wide river at a speed of thirty-five miles per hour could hardly be ignored, and when he brought his invention to England in the early 'Nineties and joined forces with Harry J. Lawson, the combination was a formidable one. The son of a hellfire and brimstone preacher from Brighton, Sussex, Lawson had already made a fortune from bicycles, and his forte was also publicity. Lawson's approach was, however a little more subtle than Pennington's. His advertisements took the form of euphemisms. His Motor Car Club, a thinly disguised publicity machine ostensibly organized to promote the motor car, in fact existed only to promote Harry Lawson. Under the auspices of this less-than-august body was organized the first Emancipation Run of 1896, from London to Brighton, to celebrate the raising of the speed limit in Britain to 12 mph. With the results suitably re-arranged to show the Lawson/Pennington products in the best possible light, the whole show was an admirable advertising stunt, and though it fooled only the most gullible, the majority of the interested public had webbed feet, it seemed.

Between them, Lawson and Pennington milked the investing and buying public of something in excess of two million pounds sterling, and reduced the embryo motor industry to a state of chaos and disrepute. They also discredited the motor car advertisement to a level from which it was slow to recover. Fortunately, by 1900, both these worthies were bankrupt and no longer able to exert any further influence.

Manufacturers and their advertising copywriters had been trying to overcome prejudice against the motor car in general terms up to 1900; the horse had been the dominant feature of road transport for upwards of a thousand years, and vested interests in both horse and rail transport were organized and powerful. The prejudice which had to be overcome was comparable with any attempt now to popularize, say, the hovercraft as an alternative to the motor car. From 1900 onwards, however, with the motor car becoming an increasingly viable proposition, the accent of advertisements was placed more upon the merits of one or other of the alternative motive powers: steam, electricity or internal combustion; and the efforts of the individual manufacturer to capture for himself the greatest possible share of the market became more apparent.

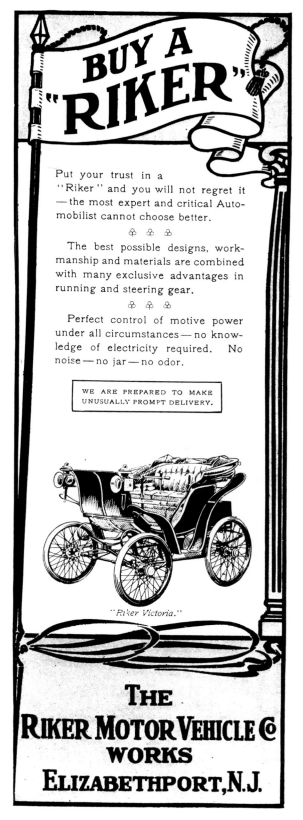

The Electric Vogue. The watch-words 'noiseless' and 'odorless' carried some weight when this Riker was marketed in 1900. (National Motor Museum)

Riding on Air

Consider some of the set-backs faced by the early autocarist: a road system suffering from half-a-century of neglect following the railway 'boom' – or, as in America, very few roads at all outside the towns and cities; smithies located in villages and towns, and geared to cater for the needs of the horse-drawn vehicle only; a lack of understanding on the part of motor car manufacturers of the need to reduce unsprung weight; a tire industry in its infancy and with a level of technology and production techniques only one stage removed from the experimental. And yet the pneumatic tire survived and then flourished, and with it the motor car.

Some of the credit for this can be laid at the door of the bicycle industry. Not only did it provide the badly needed stimulus for road improvement, it also brought the pneumatic tire into general public acceptance, and financed the tire industry to an extent which permitted more rapid technological growth.

At first, and particularly with heavier vehicles, there was a strong case for adherence to solid tires, which survived on commercial vehicles well into the 1920's, and on some steam vehicles even longer, but with the exception of the 'highwheeler' vogue in America solids were virtually extinct by 1900 on the motor car. The post-war Trojan was a notable exception, but in its case pneumatics were eschewed purely on economic grounds.

The main selling points illustrated in advertisements were initially comfort, greater freedom from flats, and improved speed and handling. Very few manufacturers – with the exception of Pennington, who claimed his 'balloon' type tires to be unpuncturable – were fool-hardy enough to claim complete immunity from failure, and if they had, they would have been disbelieved. Stops caused by tire failure were the most common of roadside sights, and the motoring public were all too familiar with the causes and remedies.

Another disconcerting habit displayed by early tires was a tendency to part company with the rim on corners or at speed. As the motor industry progressed, this problem was overcome by the employment of the 'beaded edge' rim to grip the tires in place, but this made tire changing difficult. Not so difficult, however, as it had been before the detachable wheel was invented. Then, it was the *rim* which had to be detached, and tire changing could take up to forty minutes in adverse conditions. It is scarcely surprising, then, that the

Pioneered in America by firms like Cole on their 'Aero eight', the balloon tire enjoyed a brief vogue in the 'Twenties. Here Pirelli announce their contribution, cleverly incorporating their name into the bodywork of the car. Copied elsewhere, this theme had already been usefully employed by Apollo in Germany.

Fiat 1899. In this, the earliest Fiat advertisement, Carpanetto has captured exactly the mood of the period. There is even a touch of Renoir about the lady with the parasol.

PETERS AUTO PNEUMATIC

Modelle 1911

extra verstärkt für österr. Straßen.

Mitteldeutsche Gummiwaren-Fabrik

Louis Peter, A.-G.

Filiale: **Wien, Wiedner Gürtel Nr. 6.**

Later known as the Peter's Union, this crude wood cut offered by the company in 1911 gave little indication of the quality of the artwork which they would employ during and after the Great War.

Stepney Spare became so popular, since it simply bolted alongside the flat tire and provided a simple 'get you home' remedy.

The use of motor sport as a means of advertisement for tires did not always have the desired result. The Russian agent for Prowodnik Tires suffered the indignity of being chased halfway round Brooklands track in front of an appreciative audience, by the driver of the car he had, only that morning, persuaded to fit his company's brand. The tires failed, the car almost crashed, and retribution swiftly followed. During this period it was, however, not impossible to see racing cars completing their events with tires in shreds or having left the rim altogether.

As with any other product, the proof of the pudding is very much in the eating, and as competition stepped up, manufacturers began to improve the sophistication of their own tire testing methods and frequently turned these to good use for advertising purposes. Palmer Tires made much of the fact that they maintained two heavy vehicles continuously in use, the purpose of which

Classicism rampant: it is difficult to see quite what image Pirelli are trying to project here. Boadicea's horse-drawn war chariots do not exactly conjure a scene of smooth forward progression.

was (both on road and track) to wear their tires to destruction. Even in the 'Twenties, however, there were still semi-pneumatic tires vying for business, and one of the best-known was the Rapson. Fitted as standard equipment to the Westcar, Rapsons shared with that 'assembled' car a stand at the 1924 British Empire Exhibition at Wembley, and every morning, the Rapson representative arrived dutifully on the stand armed with Cherry Blossom boot polish and gold paint and proceeded to smarten up the tires on the exhibits and highlight the name of the product. But it wasn't all show, and a good deal of kudos was gained when a Rapson-shod Westcar completed a 10,000-mile RAC-observed run in thirty-four days, and acquitted itself well.

Among the bewildering number of tire manufacturers, between whom there was little to choose, a certain 'brand image' or individuality nevertheless emerged. Normally, this manifested itself in the tread pattern. Dunlop adopted the 'herring bone' type, and some manufacturers even so arranged things that their tires spelled out the company name when driven through soft ground or snow. One or two motor manufacturers also experimented with tires, and among these, Cole will be remembered for the introduction of the balloon-type. Kelly-Springfield, the truck manufacturers, were always better known for their tires in the years before being taken over by Goodyear, and the superb draftsmanship of their artist, Fellows, was very largely responsible for this. Cars depicted in his cartoon-type advertisements were always recognizable makes, and the characters and users of the 'superior' product insufferably smug.

As time went by, the advantages of improved braking, road holding, longevity, reliability and safety were all plugged to death, and by the 1930's Dunlop had said just about all that could be said in words. Which is fortunate, since it prompted them to attempt by means of artistic evocation (page 125 and others) what Jordan had so successfully achieved by means of poetry.

De Dion Bouton 1899. Wilhio has crammed so much action into this scene that the advertisement seems almost incidental.

Moving with the times: Orio & Marchand, former sewing machine and bicycle makers were just two years into motor manufacturing when this one appeared. A good idea but the car is somewhat ghostly. *Circa* 1900. (Worthington-Williams Collection)

The New Art

If the popularity of the bicycle waned after 1900, the influence of Art Nouveau did not, and although there was increasing reliance upon photographs and standard typography for run-of-the-mill advertisements, the art form so reminiscent of the 'Nineties continued to be used in modified styles up until 1914, and occasionally even into the 'Twenties. This ensured the occasional enlivening splash of color (page 45), during a period which was to become increasingly arid in the field of advertising.

The Marine Influence

Cars themselves had acquired a bewildering nomenclature, derived partly from the strong French influence, partly from horse-drawn carriage design and,

Careful to quote their sources and thus avoid the taunt of plagiarism, one would have thought however, that the firm who invented the word 'petrol' would have had more originality in their choice of slogan. 1905.

somewhat surprisingly, from the nautical sphere. Bearing in mind that unhindered by restrictive legislation the automobile had developed a good deal faster in Europe – and in France in particular – than in Britain, such words as *chauffeur*, *chassis* and *carburettor*, *landaulette* and *coupé de ville* were naturally adopted. The last two derived from the carriage trade, as did terms like dogcart, waggonette and victoria. The nautical influence is, however, a little more difficult to understand until one realizes that, initially, the motor car was patronized only by the very rich and either complemented or replaced the motor yacht as the latest toy. Thus we find that the first motor car insurance policy written by Lloyds of London was placed in the marine insurance market, and the policy was written as though the motor car was a ship navigating the rocks and shoals of the high road. Similarly, one finds advertisements for chauffeurs 'requiring berths' and notices a strong nautical style in the dress of early autocarists.

The Electric Vogue

A flourishing business in town carriages of the open landau type had of course existed previously and these vehicles were largely the province of milady on her shopping trips to Tiffanys, Bon Marché, Harrods and such establishments. The inherent weaknesses of the early motor car – noise, and the need for occasional brute force – tended to rule out the petrol motor for this class of travel; the result was a limited vogue in electric vehicles, and for a time the landau, phaeton, brougham and victoria market was dominated by this type,

The electric vogue enjoyed a longer currency in America than anywhere else, appealing mainly to women as a 'town car'. Detroit remained in business until 1938. (1912)

23

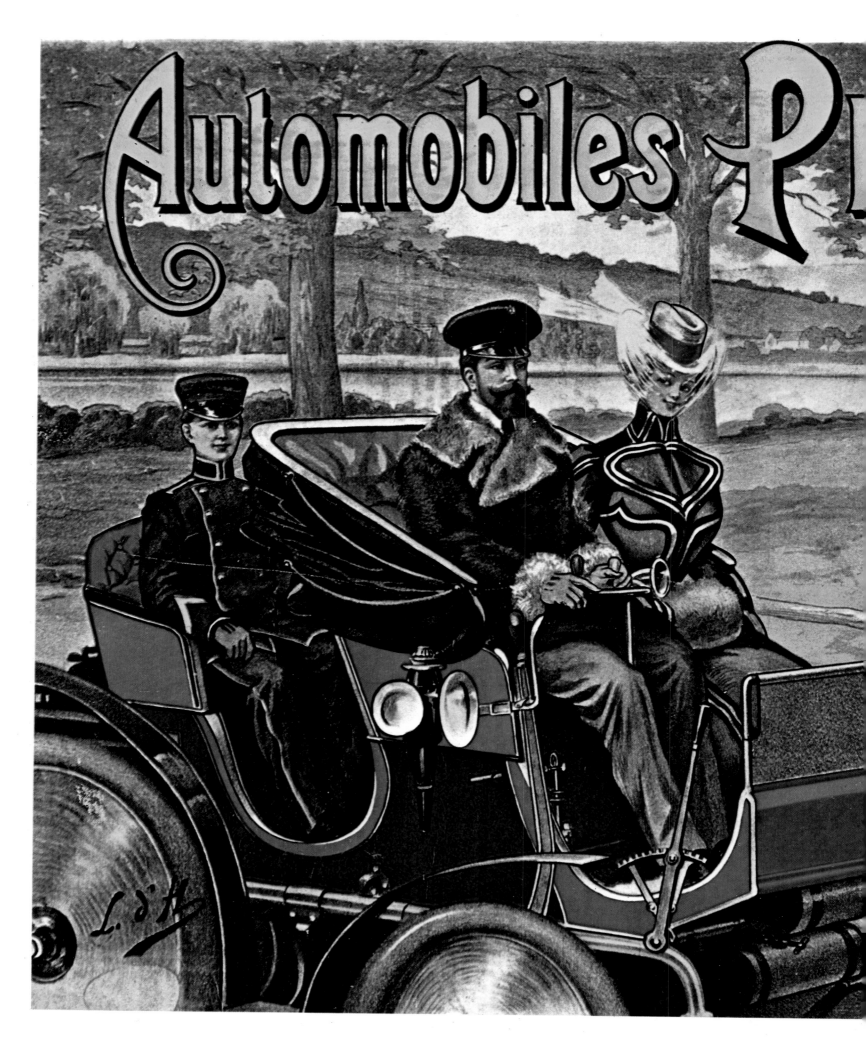

UGEOT

PARIS
83, Bould Gouvion St Cyr

IMP. du GRIFFON
10. RUE de BUCI. PARIS

More transitional: all the animation, if not the
romance, of the bicycle poster is here. Pioneering the
'S' shaped layout later recognised and exploited more
fully, Peugeot's 1899 effort was better than many.

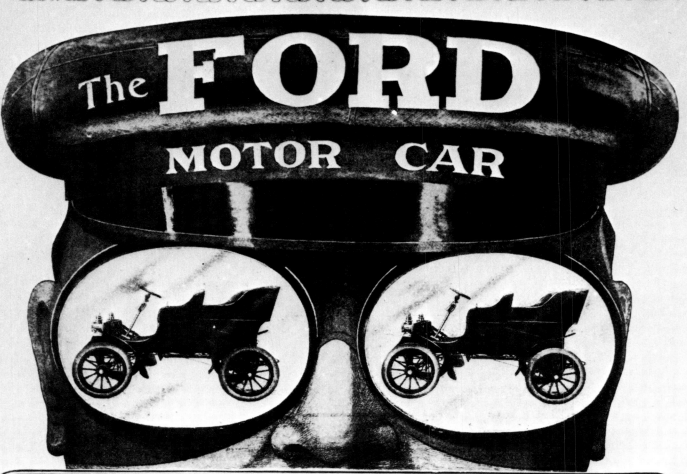

The **FORD** MOTOR CAR

In the eyes of the Chauffeur

is the most satisfactory Automobile made for every-day service. The two-cylinder (opposed) motor gives 8 actual horse-power, and eliminates the vibration so noticeable in other machines. The body is luxurious and comfortable and can be removed from the chassis by loosening six bolts.

Price with Tonneau $900.00
As a Runabout $800.00
Standard equipment includes 3-inch heavy double-tube tires

We agree to assume all responsibility in any action the TRUST may take regarding alleged infringement of the Selden Patent to prevent you from buying the Ford—"*The Car of Satisfaction.*"

We Hold the World's Record.

The Ford "999" (the fastest machine in the world), driven by Mr. Ford, made a mile in 39⅘ seconds; equal to 92 miles an hour.
Write for illustrated catalogue and name of our nearest agent.

Ford Motor Co., Detroit, Mich.

its limited range on one battery charge presenting no drawback for short trips about town. Perhaps one of the most popular makes was the Detroit Electric (page 23), although a rival make, the City and Suburban (1901–1905), was favored by Queen Alexandra and a whole galaxy of aristocrats. The company was founded by Paris Singer of sewing machine fame, who never tired of listing his titled customers – a ploy copied widely by others in the years to come. The art of name-dropping is well illustrated by the Napier advertisement (below) in which lack of space seems to be the only limitation.

Exhibitions had, of course, long been the accepted means of bringing products to the public attention, and whilst initially they provided a convenient forum for the promotion of the motor car in general, they quickly became the shop window whereby rival manufacturers could vie one with another for patronage, and provided the public with a focal point for the drawing of comparisons.

Opposite: before the flood: in the days before the Model T popularised owner-driving, even Fords were chauffeur driven. Since the chauffeur knew more about the car than its owner, he exerted considerable influence upon the latter's choice of car, and Ford recognised this with this appeal in 1904. (Ford archives, Dearborn, Michigan)

When in doubt, list your Maharajas: S. F. Edge, archetypal Edwardian publicity man, seen here blowing his six cylinder trumpet in 1906.

6 CYLINDER 6

NAPIER

SYNCHRONISED IGNITION.

THE FIRST SIX-CYLINDER AND STILL THE BEST.

40 Motor Manufacturers have already copied the principle introduced by the "NAPIER."

SIX-CYLINDER CARS BY MANY OTHER MAKERS ARE IN THE EXPERIMENTAL STAGES.

THE 6-CYLINDER "NAPIER."

A FEW OWNERS OF SIX-CYLINDER NAPIERS.

H.R.H. THE DUKE OF CONNAUGHT.	LORD DE RAMSEY.	CAPTAIN R. DUFF.
HIS GRACE THE DUKE OF FIFE.	SIR HERBERT ASHMAN.	E. R. BACON, ESQ.
COUNTESS OF GOSFORD.	SIR WILLIAM EDEN.	J. B. LONSDALE, ESQ., M.P.
COUNTESS DE GREY.	SIR OSWALD MOSELEY.	PIERPONT MORGAN, ESQ.
VISCOUNT CHURCHILL.	SIR CHARLES SEELEY.	MADAME MELBA
EARL NORTHBROOK.	SIR CHARLES TENNANT.	J. S. PHIPPS, ESQ.
EARL POULETT.	RT. HON. A. J. BALFOUR.	LEOPOLD DE ROTHSCHILD, ESQ.
LORD BATTERSEA.	GENERAL GLOAG.	LIONEL DE ROTHSCHILD, ESQ.
LORD DERBY.	GENERAL SPITZER.	ARTHUR SASSOON, ESQ.
LORD FARQUHAR.	COLONEL COLIN CAMPBELL.	PARIS E. SINGER, ESQ.
LORD HILLINGDON.		

THREE YEARS' GUARANTEE.

£20 a week penalty guarantee against late delivery with every 6-Cylinder "NAPIER."

S. F. EDGE, Ltd., 14, New Burlington St., London, W.

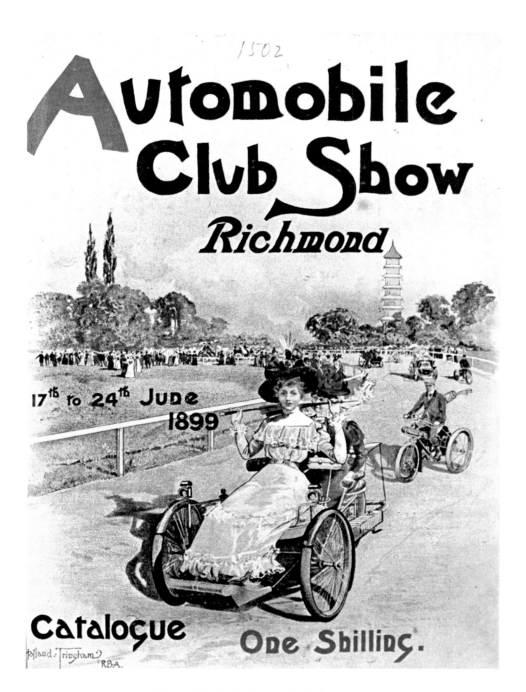

Although she looks happy, the lady 'nearest the accident' did not bring in the public, and the Richmond Show lost the Automobile Club (later R.A.C.) £1,600. Cordingley took over, but from 1902 the Motor Show has been run by the Society of Motor Manufacturers and Traders.

Right: bicycle art transitional: the propriety of the ladies in the motor car is in sharp contrast to the innocent, but nevertheless slightly erotic, quasi-medieval maiden with the bicycle. *Circa* 1902.

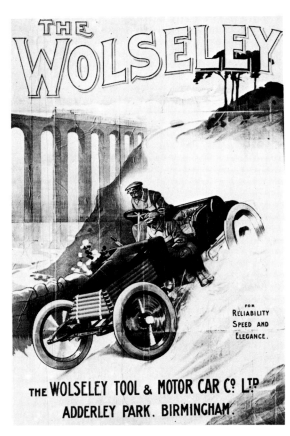

THE WOLSELEY

FOR RELIABILITY SPEED AND ELEGANCE.

THE WOLSELEY TOOL & MOTOR CAR C? L?P
ADDERLEY PARK. BIRMINGHAM.

Although few would now associate Wolseley with racing, the company was active in the sport at the time this poster appeared in 1902. It probably depicts the company's entry in the Paris–Vienna race of that year.

The 'public' was, of course, a small and exclusive band, since in Europe at least, ownership of a motor car in the early years of the Twentieth Century was restricted to the moneyed industrial classes and the aristocracy, with perhaps a sprinkling of doctors and other professional people – particularly in outlying areas – accounting for sales in the £200–£300 range. Rovers, Humbers, Maxwells and single-cylinder Cadillacs were popular in the latter category, but in America where metalled roads were to remain non-existent outside towns well into the 'Twenties, the country doctor hung on to his horse and buggy longer than elsewhere.

Mass Production

The impression might be gained that the development of the motor car in the United States and Europe was destined to follow parallel paths, but this is far from the truth. Mass production, as applied to the motor industry was not, as is commonly believed, the brainchild exclusively of Henry Ford with his Model T, although the example was set in America. The real pioneer of mass production was Ransom Eli Olds. Following a disastrous fire at his Detroit factory in 1901, operations were transferred to Lansing, Michigan and between 1903 and 1905 his 'curved dash' Oldsmobile led the sales race with production reaching some 4000 units per annum. The Oldsmobile set the pattern in America and cheap single-cylinder runabouts outsold all other types. Cadillac and Rambler were also, during this time, producing this type although the former company eventually concentrated on the luxury market, but the wealthier buyers still preferred to purchase European cars, many of whom had agents in America and who exhibited regularly at the Importer's Salon section of the New York Show.

Hire purchase – the offering of 'deferred terms' – is almost as old as the industry itself, and there are recorded instances well before the turn of the Century. Firms like Frank Peach & Co. of Holborn Viaduct, London and others like them offered a comprehensive catalog of vehicles on the 'never-never', although these were primarily aimed at the professional classes, and it was the adoption of the motor car by mail-order firms of the stature of Sears Roebuck & Co. of Chicago which made the cheap motor car just as common in rural America as the Kalamazoo stove.

A design-style native only to America, and current until about 1910 was the anachronistic 'high-wheeler'. Combining the simplicity of the single-cylinder engine with the large iron or solid rubber-tired wheels of the horse buggy, it proved a boon to farmers in areas where roads existed in name only. It was the staple product of various firms like Holsman, Schacht, McIntyre and Zimmerman, and prompted agricultural implement manufacturers like International Harvester to join the ranks of automobile manufacturers. As time went on, other firms better known for their threshing machines and ploughs – like J. I. Case and Moline Plow Company – were also destined to essay automobile manufacture, but despite the established history of agricultural activity in Britain and Europe, this phenomenon remained peculiar to America.

At this point, it is interesting to note that having founded factories mainly in or around areas of high population density, automobile manufacturers began to appear in outlying areas too, and this development was by no means confined to the United States. In this respect the motor car was unique, since it reversed the pattern of other manufacturing activity much of which had originated as cottage industries and gradually gravitated toward large centers with the onset of the industrial revolution. The result was that, whilst, the major manufacturers catered for a national and international clientele they were complemented by a whole army of 'regional' makes whose ambitions, generally speaking, did not extend beyond the immediate locality in which they were made, and often catered for a purely local need. This growth of regional companies (which often encouraged a fierce marque loyalty by the use of local names) was to continue well into the 1920's and only died out when

SIX versus FOUR.

Some facts, comparisons and reasons proving that the six-cylinder NAPIER has on every count shown its superiority over four-cylinder cars of equal or greater horse-power.

The Six-Cylinder **NAPIER** All-British.

FASTEST ON THE LEVEL.	**BROOKLANDS 1907.** The six-cylinder Napier Cars swept the board of almost all the principal events, beating cars of greater or much greater horse-power on every occasion during the season.	**LIGHTER ON TYRES.**	The Napier Self-Lubricating Clutch engages in such a gradual manner that a certain amount of slip is allowed, enabling the car to glide away smoothly—without undue strain or violent jerk on the tyres. In a recent test, based on the running of three privately-owned six-cylinder Napier cars with heavy covered-in bodies, the average mileage per tyre on the three cars was 5,550 miles per tyre.
FASTEST ON HILLS.	**HILL-CLIMBING COMPETITIONS, 1907.** Fromes Hill, Shelsley Walsh, N.E. Lancashire, Coventry M.C., Yorkshire M.C., Gaillon (France). Fastest time made in each case by six-cylinder Napiers. Over 50 cars of greater horse-power beaten.	**CHEAPER TO RUN.**	The six-cylinder Napier is cheaper to run than similarly-powered four-cylinder cars, because 90% of the driving is done on top gear. This saves wear of tyres and strain on working parts incidental to constant changing and economises petrol. (The flexibility of the engine permits driving in traffic on top gear.
USES LESS PETROL AND LUBRICATING OIL.	A 40-h.p. six-cylinder Napier, under official observation of the R.A.C., ran 200 miles with four passengers, and recorded an average of 19.26 miles per gallon of petrol. A 40-h.p six-cylinder Napier, under official observation of the R.A.C., ran 510½ miles on 1 pint 8.5 ozs of Napier Lubricating Oil, showing that it would run 2,866 miles per gallon of oil.	**QUIETER AND SMOOTHER.**	Infinitely quieter than a similar y-powered four-cylinder car because each cylinder fires a smaller charge than the four big cylinders, and therefore the explosions and exhaust are less violent. The smooth unbroken flow of six smaller cylinders is in striking contrast to the heavy pulsations and hammering beats of four larger cylinders.

S. F. EDGE (1907), LTD., 14, New Burlington Street, LONDON, W.

How many cylinders? The ebullient S. F. Edge advocates his six cylinders. He backed words with deeds, however, and had already celebrated the opening of Brooklands in 1907 by covering 1,582 miles in 24 hours round the track in a stripped Napier 'Sixty'.

Shutting the stable door: let's hope that it isn't the Master blazing so cheerfully in the back seat. Baudry de Saunier, as well as writing chauffeur's handbooks, was also editor-in-chief of *Omnia*, one of France's premier motor magazines. 1906.

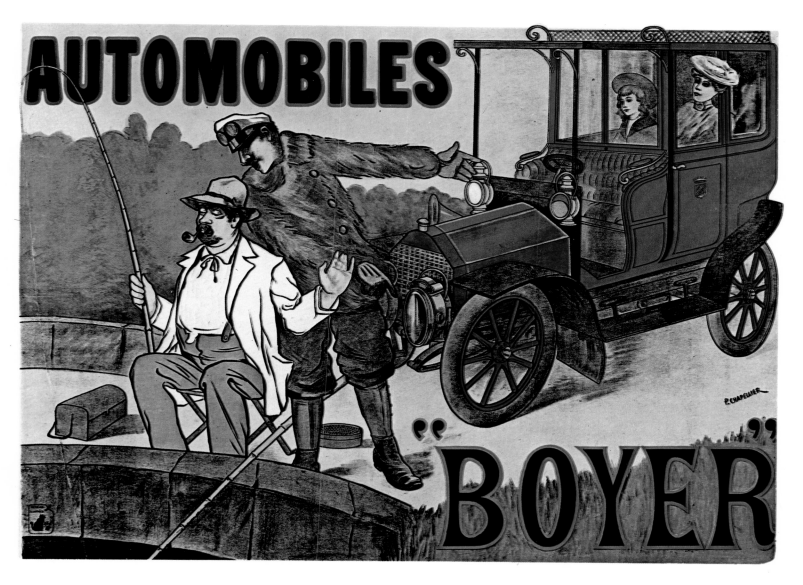

The situation is tense in this Boyer poster of about
1905. The driver of the small coupé de ville, obviously
a member of a European royal family (see crest on
door), seems to want to drive his charges round the
pond. (National Motor Museum)

Opposite: race relations 1903. The chauffeur has
consented to allow Madame to take the wheel, but
would he really have been so complacent with that
cliff edge so close – even in a De Dion Bouton?

Brand image: huntin', shootin' and fishin' was as much the prerogative of the French 'squire' as it was of his British counterpart, when this Renault offering appeared in 1908. The undertones are more subtle, however, seeking to illustrate to 'horsey' people that automobiles and horses could complement one another.

LOZIER WINS ANOTHER VICTORY

WORLDS RECORDS BROKEN

On March 19th
Teddy Tetzlaff with a
46 H.P. Lozier stock car
defeated Ralph De Palma with
his 90 H. P. imported Grand Prize Fiat
racing car in a 100 mile match race on
the 1 mile Los Angeles Motordrome, winning by over 6 miles
and breaking the World's Records from 25 to 100 miles in
the phenomenal average time of 80 55-100 miles per hour.
Time for 100 miles: 1 hour, 14 minutes and 29 seconds.

These Constant Lozier Victories

have a meaning of deep significance. Tetzlaff's victory over De Palma was the sixteenth consecutive event in which Lozier stock cars have met and defeated great cars and great drivers, broken World's Records or won National Championships. *Yet in all these great events there is not recorded a single instance of a breakdown or failure to finish*—a succession of perfect performances without a parallel in the entire history of Automobile Contests. They signify supreme endurance and marvelous mechanical perfection.

Lozier Cars Are Not Racing Cars

they are beautiful, comfortable cars of character and refinement, raced merely to demonstrate their wonderful powers of endurance and perfect mechanical construction. No other car is used by so great a number of experienced motorists—men of experience with other high-class cars of the world—who demand and are satisfied with nothing less than absolute satisfaction.

Can you afford to overlook a car of this remarkable character?

The agency for the Lozier car is a valuable asset. Correspondence solicited with dealers in unoccupied territory

LOZIER MOTOR COMPANY, DETROIT, MICH. P. O. Box 718

Improving the breed: Lozier were careful to stress that the cars they raced were no different from those which the public could buy. 1911.

standardization, sales marketing techniques, road and rail communication and after-sales servicing by the larger combines rendered unprofitable the small production of the regional makers.

Watchwords

The progress of the more successful companies was by no means smooth. Initially, advertisements had relied upon selling points which stressed the advantage of the car over the horse – the fact that one chauffeur could replace the army of grooms and stable lads which the horse required, and that the motor consumed fuel *only* when it was working. This example from the elaborate prospectus of British entrepreneur Harry Lawson's company typifies the somewhat naïve methods of persuasion:

> *Horses work for a few hours only, motors keep on incessantly.*
> *Horses shy and take fright, motors cannot.*
> *Horses fall down and run lame, motors never slip anywhere.*
> *Horses sicken and die, motors can be renewed in any part.*

. . . and so on, in a vein that would have brought the full weight of the Trades Descriptions Act down on him in modern times. Three generations ago it was powerful stuff, and pulled in the clients – in this case would-be shareholders.

The next hurdle which had to be overcome was that of unreliability, and the manufacturer who was able to convince his purchasers that they would arrive at their destination without undue incident cut a deal more ice than when he stressed only maximum speed. But whilst the doctor or farmer may have been

Opposite: the husband buys the car, but the wife chooses it: so said ad-man Ned Jordan in 1917. Whilst not strictly true in 1907, nevertheless the organisers of the New York Automobile Show recognised milday's increasing influence.

At one time the issue of trade postcards was a widespread practice, embracing everything from soap to Shell petrol. The series shown here appeared in 1908.

1st. Unsuccessful Motorist:—
"First Prize again: just his luck. I tell you what Ted we must change our Spirit. He always wins on "SHELL""

"SHELL" MOTOR SPIRIT

THE BEST MASCOT

AUTOMOBILIA

THE ONLY
ENGLISH MO·
TOR REVIEW
PUBLISHED ON
THE CONTINENT

NOTICE

To Manufacturers, Dealers, Importers, Agents and Users of

Gasoline Automobiles

United States Letters Patent No. 549,160, granted to George B. Selden, November 5th, 1895, controls broadly all gasoline automobiles which are accepted as commercially practical. Licenses under this patent have been secured from the owners by the following named manufacturers and importers

Electric Vehicle Co.
The Winton Motor Carriage Co.
Packard Motor Car Co.
Olds Motor Works.
Knox Automobile Co.
The Haynes-Apperson Co.
The Autocar Co.
The George N. Pierce Co.
Apperson Bros. Automobile Co.
Searchmont Automobile Co.
Locomobile Company of America.
The Peerless Motor Car Co.
U S. Long Distance Auto. Co.
Waltham Manufacturing Co.
Buffalo Gasolene Motor Co.

Pope Motor Car Co.
The J. Stevens Arms and Tool Co.
H. H. Franklin Mfg. Co.
Charron, Giradot & Voigt
     Company of America.
          (Smith & Mabley)
The Commerial Motor Co.
Berg Automobile Co.
Cadillac Automobile Co.
Northern Manufacturing Co.
Pope-Robinson Co.
The Kirk Manufacturing Co.
Elmore Mfg. Co.
E. R. Thomas Motor Co.
The F. B. Stearns Company.

These manufacturers
pioneers in this industry, and have commerci
by many years of development, and at a g
owners of upwards of four hundred Unite
many of the most important improvements ar
Both the basic Selden patent and all other
               will be enforced against all i
No other manufacturers or importers are a
gasoline automobiles, and any person maki
machines made or sold by any unlicensed m
               will be liable to prosecution for

Association of
Automobile Man

No. 7 EAST 42nd STREE

Politics and propaganda: the infamous Selden dispute. Fortunately Ford won – eventually.

NOTICE

To Dealers, Importers, Agents and Users of Our

Gasoline Automobiles

WE will protect you against any prosecution for alleged infringements of patents. Regarding alleged infringement of the Selden patent we beg to quote the well-known Patent Attorneys, Messrs. Parker and Burton : "The Selden patent is not a broad one, and if it was it is anticipated. It does not cover a practicable machine, no practicable machine can be made from it and never was so far as we can ascertain. It relates to that form of carriage called a FORE CARRIAGE. None of that type has ever been in use, all have been failures. No court in the United States has ever decided in favor of the patent on the merits of the case, all it has ever done was to record a prior agreement between parties."

We are pioneers of the GASOLINE AUTOMOBILE. Our Mr. Ford made the first Gasoline Automobile in Detroit and the third in the United States. His machine made in 1893 (two years previous to the granting of the Selden patent, Nov. 5, 1895) is still in use. Our Mr. Ford also built the famous "999" Gasoline Automobile, which was driven by Barney Oldfield in New York on July 25th, 1903, a mile in 55 4-5 seconds on a circular track, which is the world's record.

Mr. Ford, driving his own machine, beat Mr. Winton at Grosse Pointe track in 1901. We have always been winners

Write for Catalogue.

FORD MOTOR COMPANY

688-692 Mack Avenue, - - - DETROIT, MICH.

Left: happy marriage: this front cover of *Automobilia* – published in France for British expatriates – combines both photography and art work to promote the La Buire. The following dust cloud is used most cleverly to separate the two media. *Circa* 1909.

Pure Art Nouveau. Doubtless William Morris would have approved the pattern of the fabric. With the subject relegated to the horizon, there are even shades of surrealist Dali's 'Burning Giraffe'. Fritz Schoen, 1906.

content with a machine of simplicity and reliability, the carriage trade wanted – and were willing to pay for – a great deal more. As the late motor historian Laurence Pomeroy sagely commented, early pioneers were concerned only with making the motor car go; by the turn of the century they had succeeded in making it go reasonably well, and thereafter they were concerned in making it go beautifully (and in a less spartan manner than early models).

Comfort was judged not only by comparison with the horse-drawn carriage, but also by the luxurious standards then found in a first-class railway carriage, and many of the bespoke bodies specified by the wealthier purchasers of the motor car shared more with the latter than the former. There was only one way to build a closed carriage, and that was by the time-honored methods of the coachbuilder – a gentleman who had little understanding of, or sympathy with, the limitations of the new machine which had already made considerable inroads into his livelihood. To him, comfort meant strength, and strength meant weight. The fledgling luxury motor car therefore labored under the not inconsiderable handicap of a body which in size and weight placed an almost intolerable strain upon tires, springs, wheels, chassis, transmission, brakes and not least, upon the engine.

So the advertiser laid emphasis not only upon comfort, but upon strength, and power, and the ability to stop as well as to go. Until such time as engine technology progressed sufficiently to ensure power outputs which were not in direct ratio to cubic capacity, engines of vast literage and sixty or ninety horsepower were advocated, and no opportunity was lost in appealing to the snob instinct of a clientele among whom wealth and position were measured against the number of horses employed to draw a carriage.

With engine size came another problem – noise. No matter how grand the

Equestrian anachronism: only ten years into the Twentieth Century and the horse – normally depicted as a broken-down specimen – was fighting a rear-guard action, particularly in the cities, where this child's cry would have rung as true then as it would today.

"LOOK MAMMA, THERE'S A HORSE!"

The realization of the car you would build for yourself is more than fulfilled in the WHITE self-starting SIX. ¶Its WHITE electrical starting and lighting system, combined with the logical left-side drive makes it possible for the first time in motor car history, to reach the driving seat, start and light the car without stepping into the roadway. ¶A ride in this carefully built and beautifully finished car will convince you that its design, for comfort, convenience and mechanical perfection is supreme

Seven league boots, conical-capped gnomes, a mountainously Wagnerian background – all grist to the early poster artist. Peugeot *circa* 1907. (National Motor Museum)

Poster art at its best. The use of the wheels of a
vehicle to spell the letter 'O' is nothing new in ad.
copywriting and artwork, but the letter 'L' is unusual.
Circa 1908.

46

SPEED

The long, narrow and low-built torpedo body of the Bedelia reduces wind resistance to a minimum, and combined with the simplicity of the transmission system, makes unusually high speeds possible. The Bedelia is the *original* simple cyclecar.

BEDELIA, 32, Rue Felicien-David, PARIS (16e). Telephone: 680-22. Telegrams: " Bedelia, Paris.'

*Irish Agents—*MERCER'S GARAGE, Limited, 22, Mercer Street, Dublin. **Prices 88—104 Gns.**
Agents wanted for the whole of the United Kingdom except Ireland.

BEDELIA

Vices into virtues: the New Motoring, for whom the cyclecar could do no wrong, enjoyed a brief butterfly existence. Here four mobile coffins from the Rue Felicien-David tempt *perfide Albion*. (National Motor Museum)

THE ARGYLL CAR IS SO SIMPLE. I'M SURE IT WONT GO WRONG. FATHER NEED NEVER KNOW I'VE HAD IT—AND BESIDES HE'S SO PLEASED WITH IT, HE COULDN'T BE CROSS WITH ANY BODY JUST NOW

HAVE A TRIAL RUN

We will fix a date with pleasure. The driver will stop and start on the steepest hill. Some firms will not allow this test.

ARGYLLS, LONDON, Ltd. (Telephone— 2641 Gerrard),
17, NEWMAN STREET, OXFORD STREET, W.

Subtle soft sell: Briault's carefully worded effort of 1906 says a great deal more for Argyll than at first appears the case. (National Motor Museum)

Opposite: half centenary: Opel had not, however, been making motor cars – let alone racing cars – for fifty years when this slightly misleading announcement appeared in 1912. It was strictly bicycles and sewing machines prior to 1898.

The Pierce-Arrow

Gil Spear

coachwork or the livery of the chauffeur it was difficult to maintain an impression of dignity whilst accompanied by a cacophony of sound which rendered normal conversation impossible and meant instructions to the chauffeur had to be given by a combination of sign language and hoarse shouting. Silence of operation became the copywriter's special watchword. With one make at least, it became synonymous with the name of the car, for the Aylesbury-built IRIS is said to have taken its name from the slogan 'It Runs In Silence'. Automotive 'silence' is comparative, and the efforts of manufacturers in this direction may be said only to have reduced noise to a level of acceptability. In these efforts, the manufacturers of petrol driven cars were, of course, at a distinct disadvantage; the electric carriage was indeed virtually silent, but presented no serious competition because of its limited range. The real threat, in fact, came from the steam car. Eliminating the need for a gearbox and other noisy transmission items, it came nearest to challenging the petrol car on this count. Indeed for some time – and particularly in America, where it was developed to a level of sophistication unequalled anywhere else – it enjoyed a vogue which could have tipped the scales in favour of steam as the universal propellant. It suffered from two overwhelming handicaps, however, that were to prove its downfall. The first was the length of time required to raise steam from a cold start; the second, the complexity of its innards, which proved beyond the mechanical capability of the average owner-driver. Time spent raising steam was no great problem at first; after all, starting a petrol

Opposite: the company had changed its name from Pierce to Pierce-Arrow in 1909. By then its reputation was so high in the United States that a permanent waiting list existed. This almost lineless wash work was relatively untried in 1910. (Worthington-Williams Collection)

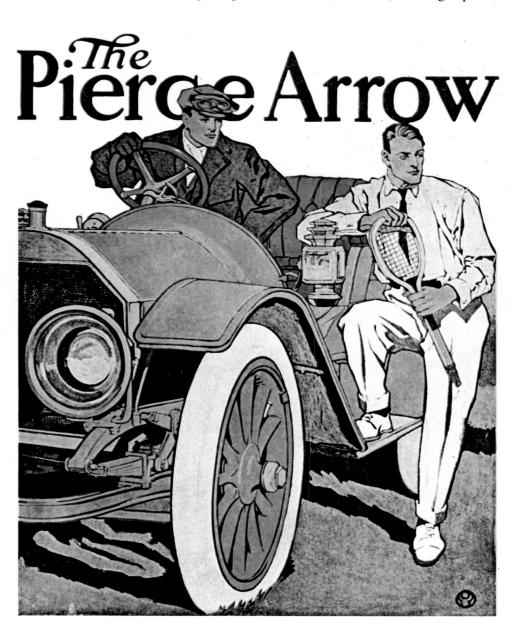

Above: silence, comfort: these were the watchwords in 1910. Now they knew how to make it go, the emphasis shifted to making it go quietly and smoothly. (Worthington-Williams Collection)

Left: anyone for motoring? Sports and leisure themes span the entire history of advertising and were always a safe bet for just about any make of automobile. 1910. (Worthington-Williams Collection)

motor car required the strength of a Hercules. But when Cadillac introduced the self-starter in 1912 – an event which provided their advertising department with some heavy ammunition – a great hole was blown in the steam car's cause. Other makes like Hudson quickly followed suit, although Ford adhered doggedly to the hand crank.

However, it was ease of maintenance on cars like the Ford which eventually defeated the steamer on the other count. Hudson, indeed, always popular with farmers, sold their Super Six mainly on the strength of advertisements which encouraged rural communities in the belief that their cars could continue to perform with little or no maintenance whatever – good psychology when dealing with a section of society renowned the world over for running their vehicles on a combination of faith, hope and binder twine. It was a Hudson

This Benz design gives no hint of the evocative and romantic artwork which was to characterize the company's advertisements following the amalgamation with Mercedes in 1926. *Circa* 1914.

Super Six which carried the Joad family safely from Oklahoma to the fruit fields of California in Steinbeck's immortal *Grapes of Wrath*.

How Many Cylinders?

Decisive though his role in automotive development was destined to be, even Henry Ford did not have things all his own way. Three years before his Model T appeared, he sought his own solution to the power-weight problem with his ill-fated Model K. Like the British Napier, which the indomitable S. F. Edge promoted so tirelessly through correspondence columns of the motoring press, through advertisement (page 31) and record breaking, the Model K advocated six cylinders in line. In Ford's case the formula was unsuccessful. However, for many years the Napier vied with the Rolls-Royce for the cream of the carriage trade, and Edge's flamboyant promotion was in sharp contrast to the restrained be-careful-it-might-appear-as-though-we're-trying-to-sell-one tone of the advertisements from Crewe-based Rolls-Royce.

Opinions were widely divided on the question of how to make the petrol engine more smooth, less noisy, and more powerful. The British-built Dolphin which had a V8 two-stroke layout, was promoted with plagiarisms of Byron and Shakespeare: 'Were Dolphin-like and showed their backs to all that raced

The ultimate in brand imagery. Had they been etched in the stone of the temples of Carthage the sentiments would have been as valid as when Cadillac first expressed them in January 1915, in the *Saturday Evening Post*. Their timelessness is reflected in their continued reappearance over the years since.

THE PENALTY oF LEADERSHIP

IN EVERY FIELD OF HUMAN ENDEAVOR · HE THAT IS FIRST MUST PERPETUALLY LIVE IN THE WHITE LIGHT OF PUBLICITY ⚜ WHETHER THE LEADERSHIP BE VESTED IN A MAN OR IN A MANUFACTURED PRODUCT · EMULA TION AND ENVY ARE EVER AT WORK ⚜ IN ART · IN LITERATURE · IN MUSIC · IN INDUSTRY · THE REWARD AND THE PUNISHMENT ARE ALWAYS THE SAME ⚜ THE REWARD IS WIDESPREAD RECOGNITION · THE PUNISHMENT FIERCE DENIAL AND DETRACTION ⚜ WHEN A MAN'S WORK BECOMES A STANDARD FOR THE WHOLE WORLD IT ALSO BECOMES A TARGET FOR THE SHAFTS OF THE ENVIOUS FEW ⚜ IF HIS WORK IS MERELY MEDIOCRE HE WILL BE LEFT SEVERELY ALONE ⚜ IF HE ACHIEVE A MASTERPIECE · IT WILL SET A MILLION TONGUES A·WAG GING ⚜ JEALOUSY DOES NOT PROTRUDE ITS FORKED TONGUE AT THE ARTIST WHO PRODUCES A COMMON PLACE PAINTING ⚜ WHATSOEVER YOU WRITE · OR PAINT · OR PLAY · OR SING · OR BUILD · NO ONE WILL STRIVE TO SURPASS OR TO SLANDER YOU · UNLESS YOUR WORK BE STAMPED WITH THE SEAL OF GENIUS ⚜ LONG LONG AFTER A GREAT WORK OR A GOOD WORK HAS BEEN DONE · THOSE WHO ARE DISAPPOINTED OR ENVI OUS CONTINUE TO CRY OUT THAT IT CANNOT BE DONE ⚜ SPITEFUL LITTLE VOICES IN THE DOMAIN OF ART WERE RAISED AGAINST OUR OWN WHISTLER AS A MOUNTEBANK · LONG AFTER THE BIG WORLD HAD ACCLAIM ED HIM ITS GREATEST ARTISTIC GENIUS ⚜ MULTITUDES FLOCKED TO BAYREUTH TO WORSHIP AT THE MUSICAL SHRINE OF WAGNER · WHILE THE LITTLE GROUP OF THOSE WHOM HE HAD DETHRONED AND DISPLACED ARGUED ANGRILY THAT HE WAS NO MUSICIAN AT ALL ⚜ THE LITTLE WORLD CONTINUED TO PROTEST THAT FULTON COULD NEVER BUILD A STEAMBOAT · WHILE THE BIG WORLD FLOCKED TO THE RIVER BANKS TO SEE HIS BOAT STEAM BY ⚜ THE LEADER IS ASSAILED BECAUSE HE IS A LEADER · AND THE EFFORT TO EQUAL HIM IS MERELY ADDED PROOF OF THAT LEADERSHIP ⚜ FAILING TO EQUAL OR TO EXCEL · THE FOLLOWER SEEKS TO DEPRECIATE AND TO DESTROY · BUT ONLY CONFIRMS ONCE MORE THE SUPERIORITY OF THAT WHICH HE STRIVES TO SUP PLANT ⚜ THERE IS NOTHING NEW IN THIS ⚜ IT IS AS OLD AS THE WORLD AND AS OLD AS THE HUMAN PASSIONS ENVY · FEAR · GREED · AMBITION AND THE DESIRE TO SURPASS ⚜ AND IT ALL AVAILS NOTHING ⚜ IF THE LEADER TRULY LEADS HE REMAINS - THE LEADER ⚜ MASTER POET · MASTER PAINTER · MASTER WORKMAN · EACH IN HIS TURN IS ASSAILED · AND EACH HOLDS HIS LAURELS THROUGH THE AGES ⚜ THAT WHICH IS GOOD OR GREAT MAKES ITSELF KNOWN · NO MATTER HOW LOUD THE CLAMOR OF DENIAL ⚜ THAT WHICH DESERVES TO LIVE - LIVES

Brand image: even if the maker's name was Crittenden, it is doubtful whether many buyers would be injured in the rush to purchase a car called a K.R.I.T. if one was marketed today. The reverse of this 1910 trade postcard (prepared for the British market) also depicts the firm's Greek swastika emblem, adopted long before the Third Reich gave it a more sinister connotation. (Society of Automotive Historians Collection)

Chatting up the girls 1912 style. This Hispano Suiza illustration just shows how democratic their buyers were.

Opposite: the aviation influence: this painting by Leon Facret can have done Renault no harm. *Circa 1913.*

AUTOMOBILES

RENAULT

with them' or 'The engine of the time shall teach me speed'. The latter quotation was also utilized to better effect (and without revision) by Capel Carless and Leonard of London (page 22), the originators of the word 'petrol', to boost sales of their spirit. Packard introduced a V12 (the 'Twin Six') of 'Ask the man who owns one' fame in 1915, and felt sufficiently secure of their position to lampoon the slogan in a later series – 'Ask the man who owes for one' (below), whilst De Dion were the first to pin their hopes on the four-stroke V8 – a power unit later to be adopted by the United States.

Sporting Publicity

Although considerations of reliability, simplicity and comfort were of high importance in promoting the sale of a motor car, the elements of speed, excitement and competitive prestige were not ignored. Initially, organized races and trials tended to be more a test of reliability and endurance on the part of both drivers and vehicles, but manufacturers were not slow to realize the value of advertising their successes in the national press (page 35). The fact that cars built purely for racing bore little resemblance to the standard product apparently made little difference, and the owner of the humblest single-cylinder Ford could bask in the reflected glory of Henry Ford's record-breaking activities at 91·4 mph in his '999' monster on frozen lake St. Clair in 1904. The opening of Brooklands track at Weybridge in England in 1907 was largely

Opposite: the influence of artist Ludwig Hohlwein is strong in this 1917 Puch offering. The style was developed in America by artists like Helck, but Hohlwein himself, although popular in Germany, failed to sell designs in Britain when he briefly joined David Allen during the 'Twenties.

Ask the man who owns one: only Packard, or a company of similar stature could afford this joke at their own expense. But even they dare not give it universal currency. It appeared in a magazine aimed at dealers only. 1915.

A new series? Yes, but nothing much. We are sure the Flivrolet will give you *more* trouble for *less* money. ¶ We *think* it will run but you can't be *sure* of anything. ¶ It's a Twin-Six to be sure but that's only a pat phrase for twelve cylinders. One cylinder will take you there and bring you back. ¶ The lines are the best we could do but styles will change anyway. ¶ The Packard has a good reputation and some people say it pays to advertise. ¶ We build a good car and charge a good price for it, to which must be added the dealer's discount.

Ask
the man
who owes
for one

AUTOMOBILES MARTINI St-BLAISE
NEUCHATEL (SUISSE)

.MARTINI.

PREMIERE ET PLUS ANCIENNE MARQUE NATIONALE

Horses versus horsepower: artists were not averse to promoting the benefits of the motor car by the use of subtle appeals – such as this – on humanitarian grounds. The whip looms large, and the laboring animals make their point – as the artist intended. *Circa* 1913. (Worthington-Williams Collection)

made possible by the pledged support of the British Motor Industry, and everywhere the basic desire of every man to show himself more skilful than his fellow found expression in the speed and danger of racing and record breaking. It was, perhaps, during this time that the concept of the motor car as a symbol of masculine prowess was founded and it was a concept which was seized upon and exploited to the full by advertisers, particularly when the sporting vehicle evolved as a production car available to the general public.

Whilst a successful season's racing brought in the trophies, it was to the sales ledger that the manufacturers looked for less tangible results. Measured in such terms, competition took on a wider aspect. The pages of the motoring press – itself largely supported by advertisement revenue – were enlivened, to the delight of the public, by claims and counterclaims, challenges and 'Reward' notices, and sometimes by vitriolic slanging matches between rival manufacturers which had little to do, directly, with the selling of motor cars to the public.

Such an exchange was the long drawn-out dispute between Ford and the Association of Licensed Automobile Manufacturers (page 39). The latter body was made up of manufacturers who had recognized the validity of George B. Selden's master patent covering all petrol-powered automobiles, and had paid substantial royalties to that gentleman. They were at pains to point out that manufacturers, dealers, importers, agents and *users* of unlicensed makes were liable to prosecution for patent infringement. Ford, who maintained that his first car (built, he claimed, in 1893) pre-dated the granting of the Selden patent by two years, refused to pay royalties and agreed to indemnify dealers and buyers alike against the threatened litigation. If

Pierce-Arrow declaration of intent, 1914.
(Worthington-Williams Collection)

Opposite: aviation influence: there, inevitably, is the passenger gazing skyward at the passing aircraft. But the overall effect is overshadowed by the presence of the private yacht and the liveried chauffeur at the wheel – and deliberately so. Like the insufferably snobbish 'He (or She) Drives a Duesenberg' ads of the 'Thirties, affluence and position are the image created here. 1918.

anything, Ford gained stature, customers, and useful publicity from the exchange, and when in 1911 he eventually successfully persuaded the patent court to reverse its decision, he never looked back. Selden's own company was bankrupt by 1914.

Stunts and Safaris

After power, comfort and speed, came the need to illustrate flexibility. Whilst Rolls-Royce deemed it necessary to drive a 'Silver Ghost' from London to Edinburgh and back in top gear in 1911, the ubiquitous Ford illustrated the point no less graphically by loading forty urchins on a standard Model T and driving it in top gear the length of a mid-west main street. No prizes for guessing which exploit was the more expensive. Other motor cars of the time were raced against airplanes, driven by children halfway across America (and by a doctor from coast to coast), conquered mountain ranges and desert tracts, were driven up the steps of the Capitol (and up church towers too), were piloted by women across continents in the cause of women's suffrage and even, in the case of Dodge, compelled to support the weight of a young elephant. This last stunt heralded the introduction of the all pressed-steel body, and following such a display it is not surprising that even in the 'Thirties Americans were still asserting that a Dodge 'would go to hell and back on its belly'.

The Ford Phenomenon

Against such a colorful and aggressive selling background, it would be naïve to suppose that the success of the Model T was purely the luck of the game. Indeed, there is evidence to suggest that almost everything Henry Ford ever did prior to 1908, when the T was introduced, was merely a necessary prelude to its debut. The systematic manner in which he first consolidated his company's position, and then bought out his major shareholders in order to gain absolute control, should be looked at in the light of his original belief in a simple and cheap car, and his uncompromising reluctance to alter the T's general specification once it had been conceived. Such single-mindedness was to result in what is possibly the greatest personal success story in any industry, and in endeavoring to evaluate the impact of the car through its advertising one is biased by the knowledge that over fifteen million Model T Fords were produced to the same basic formula over a period of some nineteen years.

Ford advertising was not very inspired, nor particularly imaginative, neither was the amount expended upon it proportional to the angle of the soaring sales graph. It was, however, consistent in its theme and copywriters could always rely on three direct selling points: Ford always laid great stress on the quality of the materials used in the car's construction (the best Vanadium steel was always employed), the unique planetary transmission (which was supposed to take the agony out of changing gear), and the employment of mass production techniques (which progressively reduced the price). In America, a country where conditions were tough, drivers inexperienced, and the mass market relatively impecunious, such considerations were unlikely to be overlooked.

Just five years after the T's introduction, annual sales were running at 248,307, and well over two million more had been built by the end of the First War. One can imagine harassed executives trying to convince the stubborn old man that there was any need to advertise at all, let alone increase the annual appropriation. With every city, town and road packed with cars bearing the Ford emblem, each car was a mobile advertisement; with over three million satisfied owners recommending the T's virtues, the employment of a sales force, let alone an advertising department, must have appeared an unnecessary extravagance to Henry Ford.

With the acceptance of the T into American folklore during its own early lifetime, the effect snowballed, and although the car was universally overworked, abused and derided, no one thought to stop buying it. The lack of a driver's door and the location of the petrol tank (under the front seat) ensured that owners never became lazy, the hand crank strained their wrists and the

Duesenberg
The Power of the Hour
Airplane—Automobile—Marine Engines

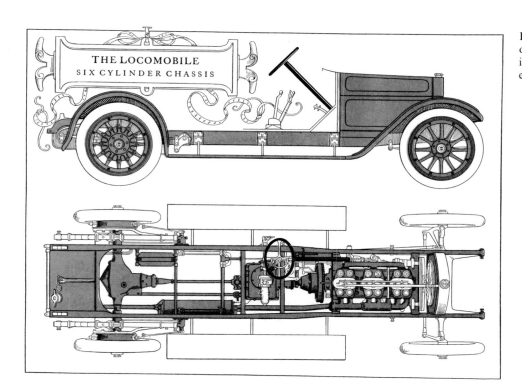

THE LOCOMOBILE
SIX CYLINDER CHASSIS

Locomobile in elevation and plan, for the enlightened of 1916 who knew one end from the other. No further information given; this was an example of restraint equalled only by later Rolls-Royce publicity.

Baker Electrics

Arriving in Style

Arriving at one's destination surely and safely may be accomplished with any automobile; but to arrive in style, as well as in utmost comfort, is particularly appreciated by those who know and want the best.

It is this exclusive factor of style which has particularly marked every Baker or Rauch & Lang production in every era of fashionable coach building.

Not forgetting that Baker and Rauch & Lang Electrics also embody superb engineering features that offer unusual advantages of service, safety and silence.

Rauch & Lang Electric

The Social Necessity

THE BAKER R & L COMPANY, Cleveland, Ohio

Popular with the ladies for its quiet running and simple operation (and probably its staid pace) was the electric car. The Baker R & L Company of Cleveland Ohio was one of the most popular makers of electric vehicles. 1916. (Worthington-Williams Collection)

Opposite: the aviation influence: an uncharacteristic study for Mercedes by Ludwig Hohlwein. The car has no headlamps and the binoculars have missed the aircraft – but no matter. *Circa* 1914, although the plane is earlier.

creeping transmission could pin them up against the garage wall when the engine started. On the credit side, the cars proved virtually indestructible and, foibles apart, utterly reliable. Ford himself encouraged the flood of music hall jokes which a less discerning entrepreneur might have imagined were damaging his business:

> 'Can I sell you a speedometer?'
> 'No thanks, I don't use one. When my Ford is running five miles an hour, the fender rattles; twelve miles an hour my teeth rattle; and fifteen miles an hour the transmission drops out.'

or another:

> 'I hear they are going to magnetize the rear axle of the Ford'
> 'What's the idea?'
> 'So it will pick up the parts that drop off'

. . . and so on.

The wily Henry realized that his car was the car the public loved to hate, no

Here we have the lot – aerial, celestial, mythological, biblical and mechanical. In addition to cars, Cole pioneered balloon tires, invented their own nomenclature – 'tourosine', 'brouette' – and eventually finished up in real estate. 1918.

The Dawn of a New Era
The Cole Aero-EIGHT

one took the stories seriously, and every joke told publicly and mentioning the T (or its various *alter egos* – 'Flivver', 'Lizzie', 'Tin Lizzie', etc.) was free publicity, a backhanded advertisement which sold his cars more effectively than a full page in the *Saturday Evening Post*.

The Music Hall image was taken a stage further with the publishing of at least a dozen 'hit' songs featuring the Ford, none of which were sponsored by the Ford Motor Company and among which were:

> *On the Old Back Seat of the Henry Ford.*
>
> *The Packard and the Ford (Rich boy meets poor 'Lizzie').*
>
> *The Little Ford Rambled Right Along.*
>
> And *I Didn't Raise my Ford to be Jitney.*

There is no reason to believe that Henry Ford was anything but delighted.

The other selling point on which the Ford Company was eventually to capitalize was discovered not by Ford themselves, but by their customers. Some impecunious owners – particularly those in the rural districts – appear to have been in competition with one another (doubtless a competition born of necessity) to discover just how many jobs a Model T could be made to do. The degree of versatility thus discovered probably surprised even Ford himself – Model T's ploughed the North Acre, drove saw-benches, water and oil pumps, powered corn mills, hauled feed, hay and livestock and generally rendered obsolete practically all other motive power on the farm. There was no rest on the Seventh Day either. Swilled out and spruced up, 'Lizzie' was expected to transport the farmer, his wife, grandpaw and a legion of lusty kids to church.

The Ford owner could also avail himself of something like 5,000 different 'improvements', he so chose, ranging from complete bodies (often of the two-seater 'speedster' type), disguised radiators, spring-loaded starters, dampers, speedos, electric side lamps (those fitted were oil, well into the 'Twenties) to tools and carburetors, whilst the unfortunate who found his cranking wrist in plaster for the third time probably needed no prompting to fit the anti-wrist breaking ratchet device offered by the Non-Kick Device Company. All of these essentials were widely advertised during the life of the Model T until its demise in 1927, whereupon most of them disappeared from the market.

The Classified Ad.

Aesthetically uninspiring though the classified advertisement may appear, the vast volume of business it promoted since the very earliest of owners made up his mind to buy a more modern automobile, merits its inclusion – that and the fact that the classified ad. often reflects the mood of the day more accurately than the larger, more grandiose, canvasses of the trade, in which sophistry could often distort the truth. This half-column-inch ad. for instance conjures immediately the style of the day: 'A handsome little Peugeot car, suit officer or doctor, water-cooled and governed engine, 5 hp, tube ignition, fast, originally cost £260. Bargain £65. 196 High Street, Poplar, London.' Or: 'White Touring car, three blankets, lots of extras, $1,600.' And another which evokes its time: 'Elmore Runabout 1902 model, 1903 carburetors, best hill-climber made, brass lamps, dos-à-dos seats $350. Box 112 Detroit, Michigan.' By 1903 as high a proportion of the automotive journals' non-editorial pages were crammed with this type of small ad. as today's. Some were advertisements inserted by small trade concerns, and here the claims were more frequently questionable. Not that private vendors were always sticklers for gospel truth and, unfettered by any code of ethics (or the Sale of Goods Act of 1896) some seemed to assume that the classified advertisement existed solely to give expression to unbridled euphemisms. Anyone who has traveled two hundred miles to view a motor car described in glowing terms by its owner, to find a wreck but one step from the breaker's yard, may be forgiven for venturing the opinion that nothing has changed.

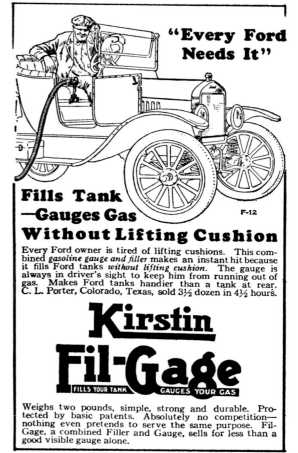

Keeping up with the Jones's. Ford 'extras'.

House magazine: an unknown cartoonist doing for Ford in 1917 what Fougasse did for Abdullah, H. M. Bateman did for Erasmic and John Hassall did for Skegness.

Opposite: pre-Czech Bohemian: in 1917, before the Austro-Hungarian Empire collapsed and before Laurin and Klement were taken over by Skoda they enjoyed a healthy reputation in Germany, for which von Loewe prepared this bold poster. (Society of Automotive Historians)

Brand Imagery

Illustrating what was recognized by the early ad-man as an essential ingredient in the selling of motor cars, an advertisement (page 47) for the Argyll (one of Scotland's few essays into the motor industry), which appeared about 1906, depicted a young girl at the wheel of a large open car with the following caption:

> *The Argyll car is so simple*
> *I'm sure it won't go wrong*
> *Father need never know*
> *I've had it – and besides*
> *He's so pleased with it*
> *He couldn't be cross*
> *With anybody*
> *Just now*

The message is not aimed at potential lady drivers, but paints a picture of a headstrong precocious 'gal', who, having tired of defying Daddy's instructions to the head groom not to allow her to take out the spirited hunter, has defied his instructions to the chauffeur instead. The disguised snob undertones are there, and in addition the potential purchaser gets the bonus of being informed that Daddy is happy with the car, and it is so simple to operate that even a chit of a girl can handle it safely.

In the case of the Rolls-Royce, the theme is handled with even greater subtlety. Built to exacting standards of perfection, the car was endowed with a radiator of classical Greek design and a mascot by an eminent sculptor, Charles Sykes. Add to that the fact that the sales were handled by the son of Lord Llangattock (the Hon. Charles Rolls) with the simple slogan 'The Best Car in the World', and the brand image needed no further inking. The success of the imagery created may be judged by the fact that purchasers of the car often referred to it as 'the Rolls', rather than 'the car'.

At the other end of the scale was the cyclecar (page 47). Quite why the cyclecar and its 'new motoring' cult made its appearance when it did (about 1910) is not altogether clear, since ultra-light cars owing more to the motor cycle than the car were nothing new, and had already enjoyed a limited vogue in the shape of the tricar or forecar. What was new, however, was the attitude of mind with which the cycle car was accepted by the enthusiasts who bought it. Unable to afford a real full-size motor car, cyclecarists accepted their plywood wire-and-bobbin vehicles happily, and advertisements, turning truth on its head, made a positive virtue of the shortcomings, spartan specifications and crude engineering (centre-pivot steering for example). The cycle car caused a curious brand of inverted snobbery – a 'comrades in adversity' esprit de corps – which pervaded cycle car advertisements and other aspects of the cult, and which sustained the whole 'movement' for far longer than it deserved.

Less happy was the lot of those manufacturers advertising products directed at the class-conscious and aspiring middle market. Some, like Humber, Rover and Austin in Britain, Buick, Oldsmobile and Hudson in America, and Opel, Germain and Berliet in Europe were content to settle for an image of dependable respectability, and their cars fulfilled this role admirably. Others of less merit tried to take on a luxury image at an economy price – frequently plagiarizing the outwardly recognizable features of their more illustrious competitors – and falling dismally between two markets. There were even those, like Calthorpe and Templar, who aimed at a market for luxury light cars, only to discover to their cost that it did not exist.

The adoption of names evocative of aristocratic or exotic backgrounds – particularly those with hyphens – was no guarantee of success either; this was also true of some of those who sought the anonymity of initials only, and thus we find E.M.F. branded 'Every Morning Failure' and G.W.K. 'Goes With a Knock'. 'Fires At all Temperatures' for FIAT is one of the few examples of the kinder side of the usually more acid mnemonics of the business. Titles with the words 'National' or 'State' fared poorly too, and all but one or two vanished from the scene before the First World War, but curiously, names of individuals (Renault, Berliet, Dodge, Morris, etc.) held their value until comparatively recently.

The appeal which an advertiser of a car renowned for its sporting achievement could include in his copy is obvious, and the implication that it was the man with such a car who always got the girl was not long in making its appearance once the copywriter fully understood the psychology of such matters.

Early attempts by firms such as Stevens-Duryea to consolidate their brand-imagery by surrounding dismembered portions of their product by columns of streaky Grecian marble, often lent an overall effect of a corpse on a mortuary slab – hardly the classical association the advertisers intended to evoke. Efforts to project an image totally at variance with – or at least unassociated with – the nature of the product were, however, not always so unsuccessful, and at this point it is worth considering one of the early advertisements to come from the pen of the American Edward (Ned) S. Jordan, motor car assembler (most

Extreme measures – like announcing 1915 models two years early – and Ransom E. Olds' ploy for Reo in 1912, might, in retrospect, appear acts of desperation. They made up in impact what they lacked aesthetically however, and the public has a short memory.

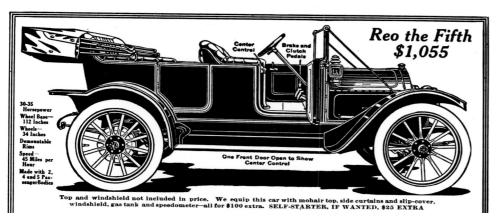

Reo the Fifth $1,055

30-35 Horsepower
Wheel Base— 112 Inches
Wheels— 34 Inches
Demountable Rims
Speed— 45 Miles per Hour
Made with 2, 4 and 5 Passenger Bodies

Center Control
Brake and Clutch Pedals

One Front Door Open to Show Center Control

Top and windshield not included in price. We equip this car with mohair top, side curtains and slip-cover, windshield, gas tank and speedometer—all for $100 extra. SELF-STARTER, IF WANTED, $25 EXTRA

The Car That Marks My Limit

By R. E. Olds, Designer

I have no quarrel with men who ask more for their cars—none with men who ask less. I have only to say that, after 25 years —after creating 24 models and building tens of thousands of cars—here's the best I know. I call it My Farewell Car.

I claim for this car no great innovation. The time is past for that.

Thousands of good men, for two decades, have worked at perfecting cars. No man can ever go much further than the best these men have done.

I believe that Reo the Fifth, in every feature, shows the utmost these men have accomplished. It represents, in addition, the best I have learned through 25 years of continuous striving. So it comes, I believe, pretty close to finality.

It shows what can be done by modern facilities, by boundless experience, by honesty of purpose, by the genius for taking pains. And that is all that any car at any price can offer.

The Lessons of 25 Years

Where this car excels lies in what I have learned in 25 years of car building.

I've been learning longer than others. I have learned faster than others, because I had more cars out.

That's my chief advantage.

What some think right, I know to be wrong. What some think sufficient, I know to be reckless.

Myriads of cars used by myriads of owners have taught me every possible weakness. They have shown the need for big margins of safety, for exactness, for careful inspection, for laboratory tests.

I Go to Extremes

For every part I know the best steel alloy. To make sure that I get it, **I analyze all my steel.**

I built a crushing machine of 50 tons' capacity just to test my gears.

My axles have twice the needed strength. My bearings are Timken Roller and Hyatt High Duty.

My carburetor is **doubly** heated, and adapted to low-grade gasoline. That makes the commonest troubles impossible.

I carry tests and inspections, throughout the construction, to what men call extremes. Those 25 years taught me the need for precautions.

They also have taught me that men love beautiful cars. My bodies are finished with 17 coats. My lamps are enameled—my engine nickel trimmed.

The upholstering is deep, and of hair-filled genuine leather.

The wheel base is long, the wheels are large, the car is over-tired. I avoid all the petty economies

New Center Control

The gear shifting is done by that center "cane-handle." It moves only three inches in each of four directions to change to every speed and reverse.

There are no side levers. Both of the brakes, also the clutch, are operated by the foot pedals. The doors are free from obstructions.

The driver may sit — as he should sit—on the left hand side, close to the cars which he passes. With the old lever controls this was impossible, save in electric cars.

Price, $1,055 the Only Sensation

My greatest achievement, in my estimation, is the price on this new car. No other car begins to compete with it.

This is due to automatic machinery —to enormous production —to making all parts in one factory. It is due to building only one chassis in all this great plant. It is due to small selling cost, and to a very small profit.

But this price is not fixed. This

initial price of $1,055 is the minimum. It is based on today's low cost for materials. It is figured on a doubled output, due to this new creation.

If costs advance our price must advance. But we shall keep it this low just as long as is possible. That is better, we think, than fixing the price for six months in advance, and leaving big margin to do it.

My Supreme Effort

Reo the Fifth marks my limit. Better materials are impossible, better workmanship out of the question. Better features or devices, if they exist, are still unknown to me.

More care or skill or quality is beyond my capability. At twice the price I could build no better car. If others can, they are better men than I.

Ask for Catalog

Ask for our catalog, showing the various bodies and stating all the facts. We will tell you then where to see the car.

Reo the Fifth, my finest creation, will interest every motor car lover. Ask for the book today. Address

R. M. Owen & Co. General Sales Agents for Reo Motor Car Co., Lansing, Mich.

Canadian Factory, St. Catharines, Ontario

Electricity has, somehow, never lost its mystery. The
demonic influence is strong in this early Bosch
offering, which cleverly stresses international appeal.
Circa 1912.

famous models, Playboy, Speedway) and ad-man extraordinary. This one first appeared in *Vanity Fair* in May 1919, and appearing as it did at the very end of an era remembered largely for its 'nuts and bolts' advertising, its sharp impact can be imagined.

The Jordan Playboy

A spirited companion for a wonderful girl and a wonderful boy,
It's a shame to call it a roadster. So full is this brawny,
graceful thing of the vigor and boyhood of morning.
It carries two passengers with a cockpit – swanky seat behind.
It revels along the wandering wind and roars like a
Caproni biplane. It's a car for a man's man – that's certain.
Or for a girl who loves the out-of-doors.
It's true – there's some of the tang of that rare old English
ale that was brewed from the smiles of youth and of old boxing gloves.
How did we happen to think of it?
Why a girl who can swim and paddle and shoot described it
to a boy who loves the roar of the cut-out.
We built one and slipped away from the quiet zone.
And stepped on it.
And the dogs barked.
And boys stopped to cheer.
And people we passed stopped and looked back.
And we were boys again.
The Playboy will be built in limited numbers – frankly
because we love to do it.

It could be the French Riviera, could be Spain. Wherever it is this Merc, *the extraclass wagon* as they put it, must have been the ultimate daydream of millions.

1914

Vulcan

Britons! Never Despair!

His Majesty's Army Service Corps use Vulcan Cars.

Order <u>Your</u> Vulcan now and assist in keeping British workmen employed.

THE VULCAN MOTOR & ENGINEERING CO. (1906), Ltd.
SOUTHPORT.

THE VULCAN CAR AGENCY, Ltd., 166, Great Portland St., London, W.

Bradford Agents: The Jowett Motor Mfg. Co., Grosvenor Road, Bradford.

Paroxisms of patriotism: Vulcan add their ten cents worth to the war effort in 1914 before sales to the public were halted.

Jordan's work pioneered a completely new style of advertising in which the appeal to the eye and the oblique shifting of emphasis away from technical specifications was to attract a whole new section of the public who were captivated by the copy. Jordan's most popular advertisement 'Somewhere West of Laramie' (page 114) was to be published in 1923 and such was its impact that the old style side-view-and-technicals vanished for good.

The advertisements became more famous than the cars from the Jordan plant, but although at first they helped Jordan to outsell most of his competitors – the majority of whom drew their component parts from the same pool of proprietory manufacturers – this company, like so many others was to founder on the rocks of economic depression, finally shutting its doors in 1931.

Imaginative though Jordan's contribution was, it had however been anticipated in style if not in graphics by Cadillac's earlier classic, 'The Penalty of Leadership' (page 51), which first appeared in the *Saturday Evening Post* of 2nd January 1915. During a period in which advertising was still dominated – art nouveau apart – by the dictates of engineers, often reading like a page from a mechanic's manual, Cadillac's dignified non-technical copy, in a type-face that looked as though it had been lifted straight off a Roman triumphal arch, heralded the beginning of the aesthetic in the hitherto mundane motor advertising world. It proved timeless, and was destined to reappear time and time again over the next half century.

In sharp contrast, is the equally famous 'Car that marks my limit' (page 67) offering from Ransom Olds. Typical in appearance, if not in content, of the cluttered mid-Edwardian advertisement, it was nonetheless an advertising milestone in its attempts to create an image of the 'ultimate' car. Whether or not it achieved its aim is another matter, and one suspects that its audacity was applauded more by Madison Avenue than by potential purchasers.

Most manufacturers betrayed more than a little of the national character of their countries of origin. France, more cosmopolitan in outlook than the rest of Europe, has traditionally held liberal views on sex and color, and this is displayed more obviously in the case of the 'bicycle' poster (page 29) and it is doubtful if any Gallic eyebrows were raised at the Blackamoor who accompanied milady in the De Dion Bouton advertisement (page 32). For those a mite suspicious of the obvious, however, consider the Delaunay-Belleville, favorite car of the crowned heads of Europe, which unashamedly used a trademark (in the shape of its distinctive circular radiator) directly associated with the company's more humble origins in the making of marine boilers.

The whole tenor of German advertisement prior to the Great War had a strongly aggressive tone, and was liberally sprinkled with giants, hobgoblins, devils and variations on the theme of Vulcan's forge in the mood of a somewhat heavy-footed Grimm.

The British managed to inject a note of patriotism into virtually everything (which escalated into a hot fervor during time of war), and often eschewed mention of all other virtues in favor of assuring potential buyers that the product was British Made – as though no further recommendation was necessary. The 1914 Vulcan advertisement (left) is typical. The Americans, with their cosmopolitan population and outlook, largely escaped this attitude but, divided into East Coast and West Coast, and Union and Confederate sympathies, managed an internal chauvinism with automobiles like *Dixie Flyer* vying with *Washington* and *Lincoln*, and *Iroquois* with *Geronimo*. It was all harmless stuff, however, and could scarcely be otherwise in a country where the Dodge (which enjoyed a national reputation second only to Ford and Chevrolet) was built in a plant located almost entirely within the Polish enclave of Hamtramck (Detroit).

With World War I, the long summer's afternoon of the Edwardian period, its art, its vulgarity, mannerisms, ornamentations, poets and princes departed. It was to be succeeded after the world had regained some sanity by a thrusting decade which brought with it entirely new problems of marketing and economy.

Masks and Pistols

Motoring clothing, designed to withstand the elements whilst riding in cars which were designed without a thought for protection from bad weather, differed little between 1895 and 1905; after 1910 both roads and the motor car had reached a level of sophistication which rendered unnecessary the provision of clothing exclusively for motoring.

Dust was a major early problem, and the difference between the eight miles per hour of the horse and the twelve permitted (but often exceeded) of the motor car raised problems which were tackled in a variety of ways. Protection of the eyes was of paramount importance, particularly to the lady on her way to a social appointment where a pair of red-rimmed eyes could be a handicap. The advocates of Ströms goggles had this to say in the turgid and somewhat incomprehensible prose of the day:

'. . . we are certain that on cars capable of any speed they are far better, to enable the human body to withstand the vagaries of climate, than to indulge in glass frames fixed on the car itself (windscreens), which always tend to work loose and rattle, and which may in case of accident cut your face with broken glass.' But judging from many of the masks and goggles advertised at the time,

Haven't I seen you somewhere before? The sight of this fellow bearing down on them in a cloud of dust was no doubt what prompted a number of Queen Victoria's country subjects to appeal to her to 'Save them from the motors'. What every De Dion owner was wearing in 1900.

the wearer was more likely to suffocate from lack of air than from an excess of dust, and one can imagine the reaction of small children to the sudden appearance of mamma in a pair.

Of the more feminine attempts to preserve madame's coiffeur, a bonnet *patented* by Mrs. Elliot Vaughan of Manchester in 1902 is worthy of mention, but whilst headgear initially seems to have been the province of the lady milliner as a natural extension of her business, it was not long before specialist firms like Gamages and Dunhills were offering a bewildering selection of hats, toques and bonnets (some of which looked remarkably like brown paper parcels tied up with string) under the general heading of 'Motorities'.

Those who could not afford a Burberry motor fur or Burberry-Proof could avail themselves of Nicoll's Quicksilver rainproofing process for permanently waterproofing clothing, leather linings etc, and for the dust menace, Redfern offered special coats of short-hair fur which, hopefully, did not gather so much.

Milady's complexion could be protected with preparations such as Pond's Vanishing Cream, still with us today, and which guaranteed to alleviate the ravages of wind and rain.

Opposite: miniature people again: this Ansaldo poster's perspective would have made the car about 30 feet long. In fact it was the first car from the Italian engineering company, a sports tourer of high performance but modest size. 1920. (Worthington-Williams Collection)

Metro-land, American style: whenever American manufacturers wished to project a luxury image then, inevitably, any houses in the background would be sure to have been lifted straight from the stockbroker belt of suburbia. Templar were no exception in 1920.

Templar
The Superfine Small Car

TEMPLAR was conceived to occupy an unique position among motor cars—worth instead of weight and new-found distinction in design and economy

To pioneer as America's finest small car and retain this pre-eminence has been Templar's fixed ideal.

The realization of this purpose is best attested by Templar owners and their outspoken content.

The Pioneer Builder of Quality Small Cars

Five-Passenger Touring, $2885   Four-Passenger Sportette, $2885
Two-Passenger Touring Roadster, $2885   Five-Passenger Sedan, $3785
Three Passenger Coupe, $3785
Price f. o. b. Cleveland

THE TEMPLAR MOTORS COMPANY
4000 HALSTEAD STREET, LAKEWOOD, CLEVELAND, O.
Export Dept., 116 Broad St., New York City

ARUNDEL FORAGE

HOMBURG

DUST-PROOF MOTOR VEILS

SCAPHANDRINE

MICA HOOD

ADJUSTABLE VEIL (Closed)

ADJUSTABLE VEIL (Open)

The taming of the shrew in four easy steps. Some idea of the dust problem may be gauged by this drastic remedy. *Circa* 1902.

For good weather, the yachting cap was *de rigueur*, and this was advocated for both male and female autocarists, whilst even King Teddy himself sported the yachting blazer with brass buttons so evocative of the Solent, Cowes and the America's Cup.

But not all personal equipment was so pleasantly associated. Quite apart from distress flares – another yachting influence – the early hazards of the open road were still well within living memory, and even the intrepid Dorothy Levitt, a pioneer lady driver, one of whose exploits was to set up a record at 91 mph in 1906, had this to say:

'If you are to drive alone on the highways and byways, it is advisable to carry a small revolver. I have an automatic Colt, and find it easy to handle as there is practically no recoil – a great consideration to a woman!' No doubt such advice was more acceptable to the American lady traveler, to whom a pearl-handled Derringer was as much a part of her equipment as the powder compact.

For the well-dressed, the Goldsmiths and Silversmith's Association offered a 'motor car' brooch in diamonds and gold for a mere £12, and for the man in milady's life 18 ct. gold sleeve links with a finely chased motor car in bold relief were a rare bargain at £5.10s. the pair.

More mundane but no less essential was Thresher & Glenny's 'Lamola' woollen underclothing for motorists, and the overnight traveler could not afford to be without Boots' solid hide and polished crocodile skin vanity cases – from 25s. 6d. up to £5.10s. Similarly, no wayside picnic would be complete without a 'Dustproof Motor Footboard Tea and Lunch Case' from Mappin & Webb (only £17.10s.).

In the days before the conservation of wild-life became a moral issue, the lady autocarist was no doubt able to wear her motor coat made of the skin of reindeer's feet and trimmed with Japanese blue fox without a shred of conscience; now such extravagance serves only to highlight the vast gulf which existed at the time between the very rich and the poor. She can, perhaps be forgiven however, for whom, with money to spare, could resist this:

'The highways and byways open up unknown delights to the winter motorist. Frosty snowy trees freeze into a fairyland of mystery that breaks into a thousand bits with just one venturesome touch. And far ahead along the road, unless there are twists and turns and all sorts of unexpected happenings, lies a long sparkling stretch of adventure. Yet no one wants to give up the comfort of being warm, because being warm when motoring is part of the fun. And now you know the reason for these soft, warm coats . . .' and so on. Enticing reading to any lady with a spare coat hanger.

By the end of 1910, motoring was not the all-weather safari that it had been since the late Nineteenth Century. By now madame was enclosed in large panels of glass, safely covered and shielded in the back compartment of her Landaulet, coupé, town car or other enclosed conveyance. The need for warmth was provided by hot-water footwarmers, or even in some cases by hot exhaust gases; communication to 'James' was through speaking tube (James by the way was usually still out in the cold) and indoor fashion reigned in both saloon and salon.

With the aerodrome at Brooklands developing almost as fast as the race track, and the exploits of Bleriot, Paulhan and Graham-White filling the newspapers, the 'in' things to wear in the new open sporting cars derived more and more from aviation practice, with gauntlets and leather helmets topping the list, a trend that was to last until the Second World War. The late arrival at a social function need no longer look like something from one of the science fiction novels of Mr. Wells, and when the self-starter invited women in even greater numbers to take their place behind the wheel, the fashion revolution was complete.

What the well-dressed Teuton should wear – including covers for the brightwork on the car. A few years later the pug would have been as rare a sight in Germany as the Dachsund in Britain.

Above: dignity for the Six: Oldsmobile Two-door Sedan *circa* 1924. Oldsmobile had introduced its first six cylinder model in 1923 at $750. At the time six cylinder cars were becoming popular in the United States and this low-priced car sold well. (National Motor Museum)

Right: Gallic immortal: it is difficult to fault Rene Vincent, and this example of his work for Salmson during the 'Twenties is one of his best – and best-known. He combines lyricism and composition with a sense of color and technical accuracy seldom surpassed. 1922. (Worthington-Williams Collection)

The feminine influence: variation on a theme. 'My Benz'. *Circa* 1920.

Below: long-distance thinking: for traversing the long French (or American) highways under the brazen sky, the Delage was *de rigeur* in 1920, with the new 4½-litre six-cylinder engine effortlessly speeding the journey. (Worthington-Williams Collection)

DELAGE

LA VOITURE CHIC

Le Chassis $12.000

Mein Benz!!

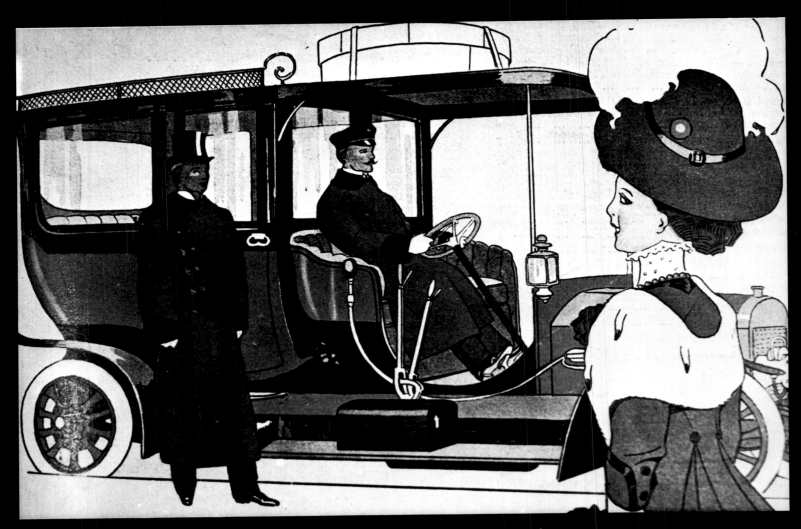

Servant wear – *circa* 1908. Was madam's hat made to
fit the coachwork or vice versa? Note the hat box on
the roof.

Decorations and Extras

The accessory market, a complete 'sub-culture' within motoring advertising, captured the energies of many a small company who early set out to supply real or imagined needs in the shape of bolt-on goods in excess of those already supplied as standard fittings with the vehicle. Although motor manufacturers themselves were often not lacking in ingenuity even in the pioneering days, their capacity for invention paled into insignificance when compared with the efforts of those who saw in the motor car an ideal opportunity to exploit their cherished patents.

The first motor cars to be marketed on a commercial basis were, although basically crude, aimed at a clientele to whom expense was no object. So far as the luxury market was concerned therefore, manufacturers tended to build vehicles – or at least their superstructure – to the individual requirements of

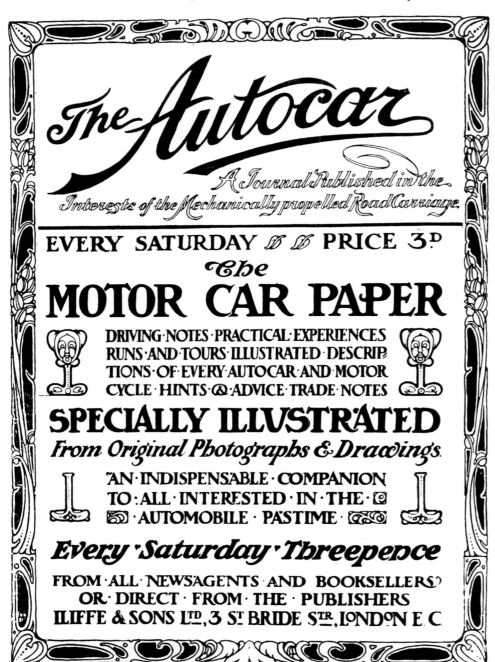

One of the most essential accessories. The Motoring Press is almost as old as motoring itself, and none more so than the *Autocar*, born in 1896 and still, with sister paper the *Motor*, going strong. 1903.

Propaganda unadulterated: this 1924 Stoewer
advertisement is from a time when the word
'propaganda' had a more innocent face than in later
years. (Society of Automotive Historians)

their customers, and there was little scope for the outside accessory manufacturer. In America, however, and France, quantity production of cheaper vehicles aimed at a more modest income bracket opened a market to those who sought to 'improve' the basic product.

In order to keep initial cost down, the first cars aimed at the larger – it could hardly yet be called 'mass' – market were spartan in the extreme, and even lamps were considered 'extras' to be purchased separately. Whenever the customer was left with such a choice, therefore, a demand was created for which numerous accessory manufacturers would cater. In the realm of lamps, horns (and other warning devices) there was intense competition, and manufacturers of these items proliferated.

With the expansion of the motor industry, and the establishment of the 'regional' make, many catered purely for the local needs of the area in which their factory was located. These were however, all basic items which had, to an extent, roots in the horse carriage trade, and for several years many firms catered both for the motor car and carriage trade simultaneously. The real innovators were those who appreciated the necessity for equipment related to the short-comings of the motor car and its environment, and who realized that the manufacturers of the vehicle had paid little or no attention to the question of after-sales service. Since the average 'smith' carried tools totally unsuitable for the needs of the automobilist, the motorist was offered a comprehensive array of equipment ranging from a collapsible canvas bucket for replenishing over-heated radiators to jacks, tire-levers, hatchets, spanners, tire-chains, spades, and devices designed to extract the vehicle from quagmires of mud.

There was also the question of safety. 'Side-slip' was perhaps the most feared of all the hazards which the early motorist could expect to encounter, and all manner of gadgets were offered – most of them quite useless – to minimize the effects of under-tired vehicles on treacherous road surfaces. Unreliable lighting systems left the field wide open to the accessory market. Even after candle-power and oil lamps had been abandoned in favour of acetylene lighting there remained the danger of lamps which blew out in high winds or

Wishful thinking: delusions of grandeur afflicted not a few manufacturers who would have been better advised to stick to the popular market they knew best. Opel fell into the trap with this Pullman limousine. *Circa* 1924.

Above: Riley Auto Robes *circa* 1903. 'In colors to
match machines'. Presumably they didn't stock
tartan.

Right: the lady with the lamp. Ducellier 1904.
Shameless exploitation of the female form – she
doesn't look remotely like an acetylene burner – and
why not? (National Motor Museum)

Opposite: electricity and the demonic influence: speed
is, however, the principal message, coupled with
versatility – in the shape of aircraft, speedboat and
racing cars. 1911.

jogged out over pot-holes (attempts to relight these often resulted in minor explosions). The options offered by Presto-lite compressed gas cylinders were designed to overcome such problems, but the solution offered by electric lighting was the only permanent one.

Starters, mainly of the clockwork or compressed air type were at best, a poor compromise, but when they worked they did remove the danger of a broken arm if the magneto had been left too far advanced. Cadillac were the first to standardize the electric self-starter (1912), and soon afterwards most manufacturers (with the notable exception of Ford) followed suit. It was, however, this tendency for manufacturers gradually to adopt the better accessories and to fit them as standard, which eventually reduced the number of firms producing such components to a handful of large concerns – most of whom were contracted to supply one or more of the motor manufacturers exclusively.

Large numbers of early accessory manufacturers could also make a living by offering parts as replacements when original equipment wore out. Whilst this practice continues to this day, it is largely confined to those firms who cater for popular models which are now out of production and for which factory-made spares no longer exist. No such sentimentality for obsolete vehicles existed

OSCAR SCHMIDT

BERLIN-WILMERSDORF BADENSCHESTR. 48 UHLAND 8872-74

General-Vertretung für
Deutschland u. Österreich

liefert den berühmten

DUESENBERG

8 CYLINDER UND HYDRAUL. VIERRADBREMSE

Teutonic America: in the year in which Duesenberg driver De Paolo won the Indianapolis 500 race at 101.13 mph it is perhaps understandable that the company should attempt to promote their product in a country where the name rolled easily off the tongue. (Society of Automotive Historians)

Opposite: no marks for artistry: spartan though this German near-cyclecar was, the absence of one rear wheel is in fact an artist's fault rather than an omission in manufacture. 1922. (Society of Automotive Historians)

Wembly-inspired patriotism: the great British Empire Exhibition in 1924 caught the imagination of many artists, and here Edmund J. Sullivan (better known for his work advertising another spirit for John Dewar) gives his own version of 'from out of the strong came forth sweetness'.

The feminine influence: the woman who drives herself.
The second in a series by Jean Routier for Solex in
1927/8. (National Motor Museum)

before 1930, and it is to Cadillac once again that the credit is due for pioneering
the lead in the standardization and manufacturing accuracy of original and
spare parts. Perhaps one of the most convincing advertising stunts ever
conceived was that organized by the British Cadillac agent, Frederick Bennett,
in 1908. Five cars were completely dismantled under R.A.C. supervision, and
the parts thoroughly scrambled. They were then rebuilt and successfully
completed a 500-mile test run.

Comfort was another area where the bought accessory came into its own. In
the mid-Edwardian period quite a number of car heaters were marketed, most
of them operated by the exhaust gases of the car; patent spring dampers and
shock absorbers also fell into the comfort category, and it was some time
before these were gradually adopted by the car makers.

With the exception perhaps of the Model T Ford and the simpler cycle cars,
the average family car of the 1920's was well equipped when it left the factory,
had a comprehensive tool kit supplied with it, and a network of dealers on a
national – and sometimes international – scale who could repair and service it.
Its owner was, nevertheless, very probably one of the vast army of 'new'
motorists who took to the road after the Great War with the introduction of
the low-priced mass-produced car, and likely to be less sophisticated in his
outlook than the owner of the Edwardian luxury vehicle. He was, therefore,

Just one of many patent self-starters marketed even before Charles F. Kettering's electric system was standardized on Cadillac in 1912. Emancipation or not, the lady on the right is asking for two broken arms. 1908.

THE BALL SEAT STARTING DEVICE

Patents pending in the United States and Europe.

TWO WAYS OF CRANKING

"This starts so easily that I love it."   "This is what I hate about driving a car."

Many progressive builders are arranging to use our device and dispense with the starting crank on their new models. Don't buy a car with a starting crank, for next year it will be a worse back number than the rear entrance car.

If you are tired of standing in the mud and cranking the engine of your old car, give us a description of it and we will see if it cannot be brought up to date in the matter of easy seat starting.

F. H. & F. O. BALL   **Plainfield, N. J.**

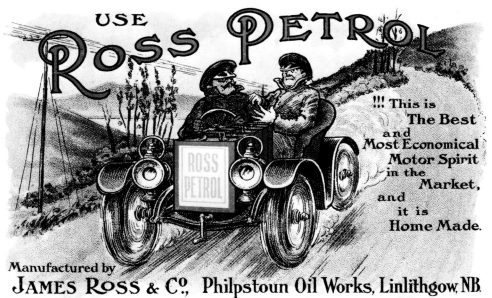

USE ROSS PETROL

!!! This is The Best and Most Economical Motor Spirit in the Market, and it is Home Made.

Manufactured by
JAMES ROSS & C°., Philpstoun Oil Works, Linlithgow, NB.

Ross petrol *circa* 1906. One of the forerunners of BP, the company doubtless overlooked the disastrous double entendre of 'home made' petrol when they appealed to another generation of Scottish Nationalists. (The British Petroleum Co. Limited)

Below: after driving milady all day in pouring rain in a coupé de ville no doubt the chauffeur needed his Oxo. *Such* a nourishing drink for servants, don't you think? *Circa* 1905.

The Reason **Why.**

How does the chauffeur
Withstand all his shocks so?
His nerves are like whipcord,
HIS petrol is

OXO

susceptible to the overtures of the 'gadget' promoters, whose extravagant claims assailed him from the pages of every motoring journal. With a patent pill or potion added to the contents of his petrol tank he could improve the performance and mileage per gallon; a windshield spotlight was indispensible; a motor-meter on his radiator cap would tell him when his engine was overheating; a muff would prevent his radiator from freezing; an inflatable dummy would discourage thieves when his car was unattended, and so on. The choice was unending, and it was during this period that the 'bolt-on goody' market established itself

Undoubtedly the more bizarre offerings can have had little appeal even to the most gullible, but even so a 'patent decarbonizer' (a small chain which was inserted through the plug aperture and left in situ with the engine running!) found many buyers, and was doubtless responsible for many holed pistons and broken valves.

After a decade of car ownership, however, the average family man was

unlikely to be taken in by such gimmicks, and the onset of the Depression brought a hard-headedness which was to extend well into the 1930's.

Just Like Dad's

Just as the railway boom in the Nineteenth Century gave impetus to the clockwork, steam and, eventually electric toy trains, so the motor car inspired a whole range of toys and models designed to cater for the boy who wanted a car 'just like Daddy's'.

In lead, tin plate, wood, and cast alloy these began to appear shortly after the car itself had become established as practical transport, and examples exist dating back to well before the turn of the Century. On a larger scale, the child's pedal car replaced the rocking horse as essential nursery equipment, and stores like London's Gamages, who were catering for adult motoring needs, also looked to the requirements of tomorrow's motorist, stocking a variety of models.

The feminine influence: Lilian Hocknell, the famous children's illustrator, could not have done better than this anonymous artist in the projection of a feminine image. The illustration has a child's story book appeal, and appeared in the *Ladies Home Journal* for Overland – one of the first manufacturers to advertise consistently in women's magazines. 1924.

Buy him a Car
just like his Daddy's
at GAMAGES

"THE VICTORY"
1925 De Luxe Model

Toy Town.

All the year round the World's Biggest and Best Toys are displayed in colossal variety in huge Depts. at GAMAGES. A veritable Paradise for the little folk.

For Town and Country use. All the very latest improvements in juvenile car manufacture including "stop and go on" signal, and folding "dickey" seat at back for extra passenger. Wired-on tyres, four lamps, windscreen, mirror, etc. Length of car 4 ft. 10 ins. Delivered Complete ready for road. Carr. paid **£6:14:9**

With brake, gear lever, spare wheel, etc. ... **£8:3:6**

A. W. GAMAGE, Ltd., HOLBORN, LONDON, E.C.1

1925 model – complete with mother-in-law seat in the Dickey. From the *Tatler*.

Advertisements were usually aimed at those who would buy, rather than at those who would use, and pedal cars tended to be featured in adult sections of catalogs, although in do-it-yourself kit form they also appeared in various hobby magazines, the *Boy's Own Paper* and similar publications aimed at older boys, and even in the *Builder*.

Germany produced many of the better small clockwork toys, and was not above giving them a political slant. Shortly before the First War, one featuring a clown who was billed as the British Prime Minister brought unfavorable comment from the *Car Illustrated*, and doting Aunts duly took note.

Unlike the real motor cars they emulated, toy cars did not succeed in ousting from popular affection the trains which had preceded them. It is, in fact, significant that perhaps the most popular model cars ever to be produced – the Dinky series – were first advertised in 1933 as in-scale accessories for the Hornby train sets also manufactured by the same parent company. The cars soon became firm favorites in their own right, and still are.

Like any other toy, the model car and pedal car sold best at Christmas, and during the shopping days preceding the festive season would perhaps appear in large feature advertisements in the popular press and in women's magazines. Coverage in father's motor magazine was, however, singularly sparse (and still is) so it would appear that then, as now, it was mother who was mainly concerned with the Christmas shopping.

Brave World-The 'Twenties

The First World War was the first fully 'mechanized' conflict in which mankind had ever engaged. It put paid once and for all to any lingering doubts as to the viability of the motor vehicle under virtually all conditions, bade farewell to the horse, brought industrialized nations to a peak of production activity never before envisaged, and trained tens of thousands of men and women in the servicing, driving and appreciation of motor vehicles.

The Armistice of 1918 brought matters to a head. Factories, geared to wartime production suddenly deprived of their lucrative munitions contracts, found themselves in the position of long-distance runners, unable to stop running even when the race is won. Manufacturing units had expanded during the war years, both in terms of physical size and production capacity. Huge work forces now faced approaching idleness.

The war had not only emancipated production techniques, it had also completely swept away the established Edwardian social order. The farm laborer in Britain who had tugged his forelock and joined the local regiment in 1914 because the 'Squire' was its honorary colonel was less likely to 'know his place' after four years in a stinking trench in Flanders, and the chamber

Soft sell? Maybe, but the lady's eyes follow you everywhere with the compulsion of Kitchener. Fiat 501, 1920.

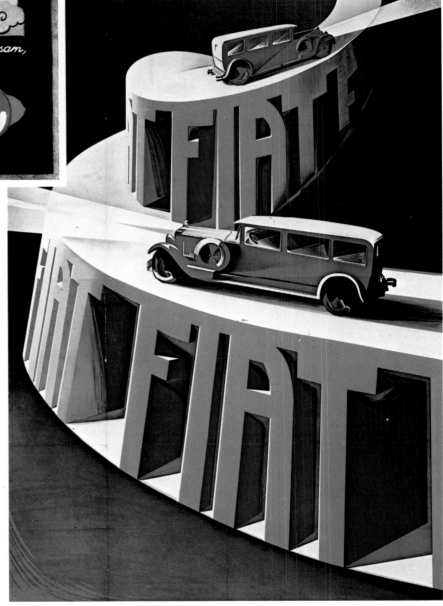

Per Fiat ad Astra : and this poster of the 'Twenties really looks as though Fiats could accomplish a journey to the stars. Overtones of the Tower of Babel?

Oriental Bizarre : former coachbuilders Szabo & Wechselmann turned to car production in 1920 and invariably their products were as bizarre as their advertising. Beaten copper bodies with hammered silver radiators were one of their eccentricities. (Society of Automotive Historians)

Double entendre: Fouqueray again, this time giving us an indication that petrol stations were fewer and farther between in the mid-'Twenties. 1925.

Hungarian chauvinism: the national colours emblazoned on this 1925 Magomobil is perhaps justified as M.A.G. (Magyar Atalanos Gepgyar, of Budapest) were one of the very few successful Hungarian manufacturers. (Society of Automotive Historians)

'You *can* go to heaven in a Ford machine' complete
with stained glass windows, organ and folding hinged
steeple. The devil did not stand a chance in 1922.
(Ford archives, Dearborn, Michigan)

Taken from the original painting in Fiat's archives,
the crude brushwork would not have appeared in the
printed version. The design is no less effective for all
that. Fiat 505 Torpedo, *circa* 1921.

maid who left domestic service to become an ambulance driver or a munitions worker was unlikely to abdicate her new-found freedom and skill to return meekly 'below stairs'.

In Europe, production of motor cars for civilian consumption had effectively ceased in 1915; in America it had been severely curtailed following their entry into the conflict in 1917, and military requisition had taken a heavy toll of pre-war vehicles. Now, a year or two after the war, the mass of young people, back in civilian life after perhaps five years, were no longer content with their immediate environs, and wished to see more of their land. The demand for cars increased, matched, for a time, by the *need* for the demand as factories turned over from frantic wartime to busy peace-time production.

Imitation is no crime – Henry Royce made no secret of the fact that he took the ideas from others and refined them; but imitation in order to deceive, demands either monumental conceit or the aplomb of the confidence trickster. Thus Rolls-Royce, the doyen of the luxury makes, with its distinctive radiator, was a sitting duck for the imitators. To a greater or lesser degree, the feature was copied by Isotta-Fraschini, Sizaire-Berwick (whom Rolls-Royce sued), Beverley-Barnes and down through Fiat, Albert, Secqueville-Hoyeau, Moon, Alsace, Roamer, and even Kingsbury Junior. The Acton-built Varley-Woods went one or two better still, with a 'hyphen' and jeweler's-rouge-polished bonnet with rivetted hinges. Beans looked like early Fiats, Hotchkiss borrowed Bugatti's horseshoe shape. Horstmann assumed Daimler's wrinkled frown. The British-made Storey, with no connection with the French-made Delfosse, looked almost identical, and the American Moon's Diana was a straight crib from the Belgian Minerva – goddess and all.

Even Packard's hallowed trademark was not immune from this treatment, and at twenty yards on a dull day you might have mistaken a Canadian Standard and Australian Lincoln, or even a Dagmar (the latter, having received a reprimand from the Danish Royal House for using their crest as a badge) for a Packard, and asked the man who owned it!

The pre-occupation with pretence continued in other forms too. The Lington cyclecar and the Kingsbury Junior regularly took space in the *Tatler* – a brave ploy which proved disastrous for both. Opel, Bell, Moon, Hillman and Humber were depicted in unlikely settings, with backdrops of pillared porticos and wrought iron gateways, uniformed chauffeurs, and liveried footmen. Even Austin, normally sober in the extreme, tried the same game with the following 'conversation' piece (a favorite style with contemporary advertisers):

Hostess to departing guest: 'I really cannot allow you to walk. Its awfully wet outside, and to send you home on foot would spoil a jolly visit. I'll ring for James and get him to phone for the Austin 20' – and then, presumably it was 'Home, James, and don't spare the *twenty* horses'.

On another occasion they tried to convince us that:

'The aesthetic eye is equally pleased with the grace and line of the Austin 20 as with the pearly shimmer of the Taj Mahal...'

and so on, ad nauseam.

Figures were either drawn deliberately small or other methods – including the worm's eye view or isometric view and exaggerated perspective – were employed to give the required impression of size, whether applied to the cars themselves or the factories in which they were built (another favorite subject).

But it was not all deception. The Ford-built Lincoln sported a Greyhound as its mascot, looked fast and was *fast*. So fast, in fact, that with the advent of

SEE BRITAIN FIRST - ON SHELL

ULLSWATER

The romance of the road: Charles Fouqueray proved himself a versatile artist, and 'Ullswater' is in sharp contrast to his 'Carried Unanimously', also for Shell. It follows the trend of the London Underground posters by Fred Taylor and Graham Petrie. 1925.

Wishful thinking: universal provider though Fiat may have been, their image was rooted firmly at the lower end of the social scale, whatever Ray Mount may have had to say about it. *Circa* 1927.

THE MORRIS-COMMERCIAL INTERNATIONAL TAXI-CAB

August, 1926   THE FORD TIMES   647

For the Travelling Worker

FOR the professional man or inspector whose work takes him abroad in all weathers, the Ford Coupé is the finest possible combination of economy and weathertight comfort.

Its handsome all-steel body—strong and rattle-proof —in rich colours, its low deep seats and balloon tyres, make it a car of refinement, and yet it has all the old reliability that has sold thirteen million Fords to the World.

It is a busy car for busy men—a tireless worker—the finest possible investment for the outdoor man to whom time is money. See it at your Authorised Ford Dealer's.

£170 net (AT WORKS, MANCHESTER)

Above: worker's Ford: well, for the professional man or the inspector, as the copy says, which is not precisely what we mean by worker today. And in 1926 not all that great number of them either, as can be seen in this picture of a town-center in Britain.

Left: Morris taxi of the 'Twenties. There seems to be a hint of the traveler returning from the Continent rather than Brighton. (National Motor Museum)

Prohibition in America it was promptly adopted as accessory No. 1 by the bootlegger – who would immediately install a tail-gunner. The image thus created was, doubtless, embarrassing for Ford, but the moral imbalance was somewhat redressed when the same car was taken up by the various police departments. More bizarre, perhaps were the mobile chapels (complete with miniature steeple [page 94]) offered on the Ford 'T' chassis, and Eccles the caravan people also did a nice line in gospel vans on the Model A.

The ultimate in the ecclesiastical was, perhaps the Trojan, for although the French Gauthier appealed to missionaries, it could never boast, as could the Trojan, that its advertisements appeared in the *Church Times*. An example of a clerical Trojan seen in London some years ago which had the legend 'I am the Lamb of God' emblazoned upon its flanks in letters a foot high was probably somewhat embarrassing to the maker (the Surrey-based one, of course).

The Aviation Influence

The exploits of the Wright brothers at Kittyhawk in 1903 had scarcely caused a ripple in the advertisement world of the motor car, but after Bleriot's cross-channel flight in 1909 – the first tangible proof of the airplane's viability – advertising illustrations made increasing use of aviation in their artwork.

Competition: P. Codognatto in evocative mood following Fiat's 1st and 2nd place in the European Grand Prix in 1923.

Usually this took the form of an aircraft in flight (page 60) and frequently the occupants of the car would be depicted standing up to watch it. The impression sought – and gained – was the association with the romance and technical achievement of flight, and of the social prestige which went with it, although sometimes the appeal was of a more subtle nature with comparisons of speed and grace and the frontiers which both motor car and airplane could open for the traveler.

This association was underlined even more heavily by aviation companies who commenced building cars, and this in turn prompted the established car makers to step up the emphasis themselves. It often took the form of inference or of direct nomenclature: Cole's *Aero Eights*; the Franklin *Airman*; Owen Magnetic's slogan *'Flying on four wheels'*; the use of the names of famous aviators: Rickenbacker, Bleriot, Fonck, Graham-White; the adoption of mascots associated with flight: Wills Sainte Clare's grey goose and Hispano-Suiza's stork (used also by Fonck and Buccialli). In some cases the association was more of a celestial nature as with Moon, Star, Comet, Meteor and Sun.

Undoubtedly the greatest aviation influence was in the application of the technical advances made during the war in engine design, fuels, metallurgy and

Feminine influence: winkle-picker shoes, short skirts, jaunty cigarette and her own Fiat 509 – truly *modernissime* in 1925.

Right: Ford phenomena: the romance of the open road as seen by Krogman in 1926. By this time even wire wheels and color options could not prevent sagging sales, and the following year was the last for the 'T'.

8 H.P. SALOON (2 doors)

Audacious Ford: parked outside a Paris *salon* this Model Y – in 1935 it became the famous '£100 Ford' – seems to be a little *de trop* if not downright cheeky. But that was the nature of the car, and the advertisement. (National Motor Museum)

Grand Prix Fiats raced until 1927, but who would have enjoyed matching his skill anywhere within racing distance of this menacing figure?

Unusu
ca

sooner
nclined
heel
hich i
on the
for our

The
is just
culating
generat
in the
Fordso
eight m

A cu
road-gr
member
with wh
power
the driv
of a lo
middle
wheels.
is the h
plate, v
ities of
road is
razor ch

The
pulling
know a
saved
away r
without
laboure
and se
pulled
which
forest la
necessa
son wil
width,
hitch or
ample

Ford
for pro
way pla
compre
quarrie
idea is
constru
noise of
main r

Gallic simplicity: reminiscent of Peugeot advertisements during the same period is this pleasing line drawing for the 1923 Benjamin. (National Motor Museum)

Opposite: feminine influence: shades of Beardsley again.

Type 5 cv.
moteur
Benjamin - Duplex

Type 10 cv.
moteur
Benjamin - Triplex

SES CYCLECARS.
SES VOITURETTES..
SES QUATRE PLACES

Lexicon: even Alfa-Romeo managed to put their name to a motor car.

Right: sports theme: once again the speed and elegance of fast sport hovers over the implied similar characteristics of the car – this time Mercedes-Benz, between wars.

Fisherman's tale: whilst the presence of the respectable middle-aged couple in this L Type M.G. Magna may have indicated that the Abingdon company was hoping to expand into that market, the fact was that open cars of the type were designed for a younger generation. (Society of Automotive Historians)

Below: Champion canary: America in 1935 was just emerging from the worst of the depression and Roosevelt's New Deal had had two years in which to help the recovery. No doubt this rather highly colored Champion from Studebaker was intended to reflect the prevailing note of optimism. (Society of Automotive Historians)

THE BIGGEST THRILL IN THE WORLD IS TO OWN A *Champion*

Studebaker Sedan
FOR SIX PASSENGERS

production techniques – all of which were exploited by advertising copywriters during the period. And perhaps it is only natural that France, whose Voisins and Hispano Suizas represented all that was best in aircraft derivation, should attempt seriously to build motor cars driven by the propellor screw – the Helice and the Leyat.

The Feminine Influence

With hindsight one can see that it was obvious that women should exert a powerful influence on the motor car and its advertisement in the decade which immediately followed World War I.

The cause of women's suffrage had been vindicated by the role played by women during the war, and most of them had either received, or were destined to receive, the vote. And with it came recognition that the hand that once only rocked the cradle now held the steering wheel and ruled enough of the family budget to influence car-buying trends.

Manufacturers at both ends of the scale made determined efforts to sell motor cars direct to women (illustration below, and others) with firms as far removed as Fiat, Sizaire-Berwick and Willys Overland regularly taking space in women's magazines like *Vogue*, the *Ladies Home Journal*, *McCalls*, and *Vanity Fair*. Color options were extended to appeal to feminine tastes and

Feminine influence: André Citroën's answer to Henry Ford, and the car he advertised from the Eiffel Tower. The distinctive badge alluded to Citroën's distinctive herringbone gear cutting in the back axle. Here Pierre Louys depicts the 1924 5CV – a favorite with the fair sex.

assumed exotic names which did their best to disguise the fact that they were drawn from the same spectrum as traffic lights, military uniforms and the paint on the doors of council houses. You could have egg-shell blue, mahogany maroon, Venetian green and South Sea turquoise; and under this invasion even Henry Ford eventually capitulated, and offered more than just black.

The Biddle Motor Car Company of Philadelphia went further, and commissioned a woman to design their bodywork, and Pathfinder (USA) employed Miss Nellie Prendergast with her army of sales ladies to sell their cars. In Scotland, Arrol-Johnston went the whole hog and put the Kirkcudbright factory, which produced their smaller Galloway models, in the sole charge of Dorothee Pullinger, the daughter of their chief designer, and staffed the factory almost entirely with women.

Ned Jordan who was, as we have seen, something of a visionary in such matters, sagely remarked as early as 1917 that 'while men buy cars, women choose them'. Steinbeck said it more bluntly: 'Watch the woman's face. If the woman likes it, we can screw the old man.' In a paper on the subject of selling cars to women, Jordan went on, 'There is just as much reason why a woman should want to see herself in a mirror when she appears in a new car as when she appears in her new gown' and there, really, was the secret revealed. Whilst the man might look for mechanical refinement or just honest-to-goodness

Egyptian influence: unremitting individualism characterized everything to emerge from Gabriel Voisin's works at Issy-les-Moulineaux and his advertising was no exception. The discovery of Tutankhamun's tomb in 1923 is reflected in this sphinx-like design of 1924. (National Motor Museum)

Competition: reminiscent of the work of the great F.
Gordon Crosby, Nockolds nevertheless had his own
distinctive style and here evokes perfectly the
atmosphere of Brooklands at speed.

Selling serpent: 'Nessy' has been the butt of cartoonists and the boon of advertisers from Cutty Sark to Cadbury's. Here is John Reynolds' version for Shell. 'Knock-less' is a nice touch. *Circa* 1934.

Rivierra reverie: Georges Ham in romantic mood for the 1934 Monaco Grand Prix.

109

Rickenbacker

A · CAR · WORTHY · OF · ITS · NAME

THE outstanding characteristic of any 8 cylinder motor is acceleration. We point with pride to the Rickenbacker performance on that score.

FOR magical action, and an exquisite sensation, a free flowing, abundant, unhampered power, you will find the Rickenbacker 8 a joy to drive.

Famous "Six" Prices				Vertical "Eight" Prices	
Sport Phaeton	- - $1595		f. o. b. Detroit —	Sport Phaeton	- - $2195
Coupe	- - 2095		plus war tax	Coupe	- - 2695
Sedan	- - 2195			Sedan	- - 2795

RICKENBACKER MOTOR COMPANY
DETROIT, MICHIGAN

Ford Touring Car $295

OF all the times of the year when you need a Ford car, that time is NOW!

Wherever you live—in town or country—owning a Ford car helps you to get the most out of life.

Every day without a Ford means lost hours of healthy motoring pleasure.

The Ford gives you unlimited chance to get away into new surroundings every day—a picnic supper or a cool spin in the evening to enjoy the countryside or a visit with friends.

These advantages make for greater enjoyment of life—bring you rest and relaxation at a cost so low that it will surprise you.

By stimulating good health and efficiency, owning a Ford increases your earning power.

Buy your Ford now or start weekly payments on it.

transportation, to a woman a car was just an extension of her personal wardrobe – it had to look *right*. And if it meant the upholstery matching her eye-shadow and the paint job her new dress, that's what Jordan would give her.

Other manufacturers took the matter a stage further. If Cadillac's self-starter had removed the largest physical and social obstacle for the woman driver, then the conventional gearbox presented the next hurdle. Chandler made great play in their advertisements of their 'Traffic Transmission' – an early form of automatic – and Premier tried too with the Cutler-Hammer Magnetic Gear Shift, whilst Ford's Coupelet – 'clean enough for women to drive' – capitalized on the 'pedals-to-push' planetary transmission.

So women became automobilists in their own right, and began the new trend in automobile advertisement, Family Appeal, which was to reach full flower in the 'Thirties and 'Forties.

The Influence of the 'Assembled' Car

The 'assembled' car was nothing new in 1919, particularly in America, and the practice of 'buying out' components existed wherever motor car manufacture was undertaken without the benefit of foundry and gear-cutting facilities. Generally, such manufacturers purchased the larger components from outside suppliers, together with specialized items like lamps and tires, and relatively early on firms like Malicet et Blin and Thorneycroft were supplying chassis, while engines were supplied by Aster, Dorman, White & Poppe, Fafnir, Herschell-Spillman, Continental, Buda, Chapuis Dornier and Fivet and others. The ex-munitioneer who aspired to genuine automobile manufacture, however required two things – money and foundry facilities. If he had neither, then 'assembly' was the only answer.

The result was inevitable. Hundreds of firms sprung up in all manufacturing countries; all of them building 'scissors and paste' cars, from components almost all of which were purchased from a pool of proprietary manufacturers. In publicity terms this meant a succession of uninspired advertisements doing their best to extol the virtues of uninspired cars, none of which differed in much

Agricultural influence: Henry Ford, Thomas Edison and Harvey Firestone were all enthusiastic out-of-doors men, given to camping even in late middle age. Whilst the appeal pictorially here is to the farmer, the text propounds Ford's own personal philosophies on the outdoor life and improving the lot of the individual. The car was incredibly cheap. 1924. (Ford archives, Dearborn, Michigan)

Opposite: aviation influence: the Rickenbacker endeavored to capitalize on the reputation of its namesake, already well known as a racing driver and Great War air ace. It was a good car nevertheless. 1924.

Ocean liner mandatory: Offelsmeyer's version for
Mercedes-Benz. *Circa* 1928.

Opposite: on a pedestal: good hill climber though the
514 may have been, this is nevertheless pure fantasia.
There are overtones of E. McKnight Kauffer and the
searchlights are pure Twentieth Century Fox.
Codognatto. 1929.

more than name and radiator shape from their immediate competitors.

For possibly the first time, both sellers and buyers found themselves in the same quandry: how to distinguish one from another in terms of merit, price and appeal. In France, a number of cyclecar and light car builders solved the problem by shuffling the components round so that in the end, engine, driver, and in some cases, transmission appeared in what were supposed to be new and exciting places. The conventionalists however, on both sides of the Atlantic, looked to imaginative advertising and it was Jordan and those like him, who succeeded. His 'Somewhere West of Laramie' (below) Playboy model advertisement became one of the Commandment Tablets of Madison Avenue, although it is worthwhile remembering that, when it first appeared in the *Saturday Evening Post* on June 23rd 1923, it was but one of the successful series from Jordan's pen. Here are some others, all classics, though not so well-known as 'Laramie':

Somewhere West of Laramie

SOMEWHERE west of Laramie there's a broncho-busting, steer-roping girl who knows what I'm talking about. She can tell what a sassy pony, that's a cross between greased lightning and the place where it hits, can do with eleven hundred pounds of steel and action when he's going high, wide and handsome.

The truth is—the Playboy was built for her.

Built for the lass whose face is brown with the sun when the day is done of revel and romp and race.

She loves the cross of the wild and the tame.

There's a savor of links about that car—of laughter and lilt and light—a hint of old loves—and saddle and quirt. It's a brawny thing—yet a graceful thing for the sweep o' the Avenue.

Step into the Playboy when the hour grows dull with things gone dead and stale.

Then start for the land of real living with the spirit of the lass who rides, lean and rangy, into the red horizon of a Wyoming twilight.

The sacred cow of Madison Avenue: it is said that Ogilvie and Mather made all their apprentice advertising executives learn it by heart. 1923.

I Want to be Happy

There is still a country where a cowboy
can spread his loop without getting it
caught in a fence post – where the mountains
tickle the sky and ten million stars just
almost scare you.

Give me a horse or a car that has a little of
the lighted match and stick of dynamite
about it. Give me a little more health than
there is in the daily dozen – a little more air
than you will find in Atlantic city – and a lot
more poetry than I ever found in Browning.

I want to go in a Playboy. Then I'll be happy

Jordan Motor Car Company Inc. Cleveland, Ohio.

or:

A Million Miles from Dull Care

Somewhere far beyond the
place where men and women and motors
race through canyons of the town –
somewhere on the top of the world –
there is a peak which dull care has
never climbed.

You can go there light-hearted in a
Jordan Playboy – for it's always happy
in the hills.

A car for a man's man – that's certain

Or the girl who loves to take the open road with top
down, in the summer time.

Lighter than any on the road, for
its wheelbase, rare in beauty and
supremely balanced, as a fine car
must be – distinctive as only a car of
personality can be – the Playboy is an
apt companion for all Americans who
dare never to grow old.

or:

Strangely we have always underestimated
the Playboy demand.

We have never built enough.

But we never will – you may be
assured.

There's too much real fun in building
a few less than the people want.

It's friendly, human – you know – to
want to have something the other
fellow can't get.

Frankly, the Playboy is built for those
admirable people of good taste, who
know how to distinguish high quality
from extravagance – those rare individuals
to whom experience affords possession of the
pride of economy, which is just another name for
commonsense.

Temple of Solomon and miniature people. Call it artist's licence if you like, but no production Renault ever looked quite like this, and even if it had, it would have been unlikely to find itself in this setting. *Circa* 1935.

PERFECT CONTROL

Land of hope and glory: just so long as British policemen are wonderful and red double deckers still run in Regent Street, surely the sun won't set? Dunlop being British in April 1935.

Opposite: by Dearborn out of Strasbourg: it seems unlikely that the Paris *Opéra* ever carried an advertisement for Matford (Mathis/Ford) as this cover to *La Revue* of 1936 would have us believe. (Society of Automotive Historians)

Which of you admirable people of good taste would not have felt, on reading such stirring stuff, compelled to rush out and buy one? The fact that the purchaser could get exactly the same specification from any one of a hundred other 'assemblers' just did not occur to most.

In Britain, Morris and Clyno led the field, and although their advertising lacked a Jordan touch, they sold their cars on copy which extolled dependability, coupled with good value. The only excitement which their advertising ever provoked related to the 'price war' in which both became engaged (reluctantly, one suspects) and which was eventually to bring about Clyno's downfall.

The Sporting Influence

All aspects of 'sporting' life were taken up enthusiastically to promote the motor car – the romance of the open road, picnics, camping, touring, the squash court, tennis party, golf course and the motor track itself. The overall impression for which advertising aimed in both artwork and copy was one of

Framed: the radiator theme was used by a number of manufacturers, including Georges Irat (1925) and Morris, on the cover of their house magazine in 1924. During the period when the radiator was the most recognizable feature of a car this was a logical development. (National Motor Museum and British Leyland Motor Corporation)

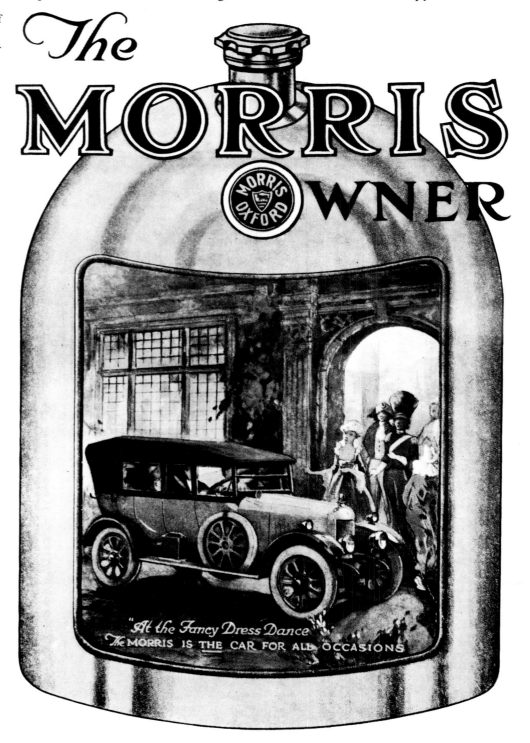

118

an endless Public Holiday with generous helpings of sunshine, expensive
suburban homes, pretty 'flappers', glowing health, and formal evening dress,
with the theatre and all aspects of sophisticated leisure travel thrown in for
good measure. A useful camouflage for the labour unrest, strikes, political
upheavals, and economic crises by which the 'Twenties were also dominated.

Gaiety and laughter were the watchwords, pleasure and leisure the facets
upon which the advertisers concentrated, and if it all seemed somewhat
decadent, it was of no concern to those who needed to capitalize upon the
mood whilst it lasted. For tennis and golf and Brooklands, the only way to
travel was in an open car. The tourer (pages 106, 111 and others) and the open
coupé with 'dickey' or 'rumble' seats came into their own, and not a few
advertisers made play of the 'extras': in the form of golf bags, cameras, and
other out-door essentials with which their products came ready-equipped.

But by the late 'Twenties the somewhat naïve pre-occupation of advertising
departments with health and the outdoor life, excepting those marques which
relied on sales of sports or open cars almost exclusively, began to be played out.

Copywriter's licence: in fact, road racing had been banned in Britain since the mid-'Twenties so this B.R.D.C. poster is a little misleading. Donington was, however, the nearest thing to racing on public roads.

Right : this Rigobaldi rendering of 1935 was in line with the contemporary image of Italy – the time of Colonialism and a sort of reinforced-concrete renaissance. Shades of the historic past can be seen in silhouette.

Censorship: whilst British poster artists were governed by the Censorship Committee of the United Billposter's Association, the Italians were subjected to the scrutiny of a more rigorous arbitrator – the Vatican. Dudovich invoked Papal disapproval with this original version, which showed an all-too inflaming line of buttock! 1934.

122

All-weather equipment for the open car became a selling point. For the others who had discovered that an open car is no asset in a howling blizzard, the cry was now for sedans, saloons, closed coupés and limousines.

Social Influence

Changing social attitudes and structures were to have a profound influence upon the motor car and the way in which it was advertised, and the copywriter who ignored them did so at his peril.

The advertiser trod warily. Awareness of the sensitivity of the market was a tacit requirement, and possibly one of the reasons for the accent on sporting activity: traditionally an area where class barriers could be crossed. However, different manufacturers reacted in different ways. Some tried a complete about-face, turning away from the markets they knew before the war. Thus we find British Ensign producing a luxury car to compete with Rolls-Royce (they were back in the £100 car class with the Gillett by the mid-'Twenties), whilst others attempted a compromise, like Rolls-Royce themselves, who introduced the 3·1 litre 20 with a direct appeal to the professional class. Armstrong-Siddeley, always an upper-middle class marque, hedged their bets with an economy car, but they were careful to call it the Stoneleigh to avoid any social stigma attaching to their regular product.

Those who did best were the ones who stuck to what they knew best, or who fielded a range which, although comprehensive, remained saleable in reason-

Opposite: mythological giant: Plinio Codognatto for Fiat (1925). The theme was pursued energetically in Germany, but seldom in Britain.

Competition: success in competition elevated the Lea-Francis from the ranks of the common assembled car in which it had commenced its career in 1920. This advertisement dates from about 1926. (National Motor Museum)

LEA-FRANCIS
Holds the Blue Riband of the Road

WINNER of OVER 100 AWARDS

Helvetian Rolls-Royce: bearing in mind the status
which the Pic-Pic (Piccard-Pictet) enjoyed in its native
Switzerland it might be thought that the lighthearted
situation here was a little too humorous. Certainly it
would not have done for Derby. (Society of
Automotive Historians)

There'll always be an England: Hitler may be
up to his tricks in Germany but we've still got
our fortresses. Dunlop instilling pre-Munich
confidence in 1937 and echoing London
Underground posters of an earlier era.

Who's for tennis? It could be Surbiton or
Sunbury but the Austin Seven 'Ulster' was
sufficiently ubiquitous even for
stockbroker's tudor. Dunlop still ebullient
in May 1938.

able numbers in the various respective markets. In the first category were firms like Buick, Hudson, Citroën, Morris, and Ford; in the second, Austin, Renault, Daimler, Opel and the like. The Americans differed in that they tended to choose a slot in the market into which all their products would fit; the assemblers were limited to one, or perhaps two basic models for obvious reasons.

Some firms would have liked to change their image – George Lanchester tried hard to ditch the Lanchester's 'dowager' image (shared uneasily with Daimler) or at least modify it with a smaller car, but his fellow-directors would not hear of it.

The changing social order affected other areas too. The *Car Illustrated*, which had been founded in 1902, and which built its reputation on being a sort of motoring edition of the *Tatler*, found itself on unsure ground. The class of reader at whom the magazine (and its advertisements) had originally been aimed, was no longer so large, or affluent enough to sustain it, and the name was changed to *Car & Golf*. It fell between two markets, but struggled on for a few years.

One car that would never have advertised in it, however, was the Jowett, and here the 'regional make' policy is to be seen once again. The Jowett was one of the regional makes that made good and developed, but until the 'Forties remained uncompromisingly spartan in specification, reliable in operation and down-to-earth in advertising and attitude.

When in August 1923, the *Autocar* wrote patronizingly: 'Somewhere about ten years ago there began to filter down to the South strange tales from Bradford (in Yorkshire) of a car of infinitesimally small engine size, but astounding power and longevity,' the Jowett advertising department countered crisply by couching their Motor Show advertisements in the pure dialect of the Dales and headed one 'Oop for t'Show'. At times, however, they showed themselves capable of the lyricism of Laurie Lee and the psychology of Jordan, and the following is wholly illustrative of their style:

'The purr of the Jowett Seven is music to the lover of roads. It sings a symphony of comradeship, this adventurous hill-loving car for two. Listen to its song:

'Step on the pedal, my master; the town's behind, the steep hill ahead. We've broken bounds, we're free! Ahead the dale and stream, pinewood and hill. For us the zest of the wind on the heights, the gleam on the placid lake.

'Step on the pedal, my master, mountains are molehills today – wheels are wings. Ah! – now you are silent; it's now that you hear me, and feel the romance in my song. I love to think of you two behind – my master at the wheel, mistress by his side. You two shall wish to ride forever thus, and before the shadows lengthen and the violet deepens on the Hill you shall experience a new understanding of joy.

'So step on the pedal; gently – for I shall respond to your lightest wish, almost to your very thoughts. And so – softly over the hill in the sunset glow – home with the stars tonight.'

It is all there, the romance of the open road, the family, the dependability – all the attributes of the successful 'Twenties advertisement. Two-cylinder teacup-sized engines they may have had, but they sold faster than Benjamin and Willie Jowett could make them. And it was not always on the same advertising formula; at times their prose verged on the biblical, at others it was blunt and homely. Above all, it was honest, and when Jowett's said:

'Jowetts never wear out; they are left to the next of kin' it was as near to the truth as advertisers' licence will allow.

In Europe the Jowett epitomized, with the Austin Seven, the Standard (page 85), the Opel 'Laubfroch', the Citroën 5CV (page 106) and the Morris, Clyno and Ford, the era of the motor car for Mr. Everyman. They were the ones who provided motoring for the millions and many of them survived the Wall Street 'crash' in 1929 and the depression which followed it.

la nouvelle
"marche à l'étoile"
de l'automobiliste

SPIDOLÉINE . LE LUBRIFIANT DE SÉCURITÉ.

Brave new world: Nouvelliere's work follows very closely the influence of Cassandre's posters for the French Railways toward the end of the 'Twenties. It was a style against which established reactionaries like Sir Frank Brangwyn R.A. fought vigorously. 1927. (National Motor Museum)

Favorite 'Thirties theme: Dorniers and Short
Sunderlands about to splash-down were much used
as backcloth for the more upmarket automobile. In
this subtle 1938–9 Mercedes-Benz ad., the headlamps
are pure '38 but surely the grille-shape dates from
several years earlier?

This 1939 Plymouth shared body pressings with other
Chrysler models but had its own radiator-grille and
trim. Two models were marketed in the U.S., the
Roadking and the De Luxe (in Britain the Chrysler
Wimbledon or Kew Six). This drink-and-drive ad.
would not be acceptable today. (National Motor
Museum)

Dream World-The 'Thirties

Inevitably the Depression was the dominating influence in automotive production in the early 'Thirties. The period was not kind to motor manufacturers. The devastating economic scythe missed some manufacturers in its world-wide swing – the ones with the right formula for the day – but so sudden had been the plunge from apparent prosperity into financial crisis that those caught on the wrong foot never had time to recover. The 'assemblers' were decimated. Existing, as they did, in rented premises and with no need for expensive machinery they found themselves with few assets to mortgage, and few customers.

Many of the larger companies who had existed for years in a comfortable niche in the market with a steady and unspectacular sales record suddenly lost their profit margin and had accumulated insufficient reserves to tide themselves over an extended period.

Those of the public who were still buying, required assurance not only that the car they purchased was of good value, but that its manufacturers would still

Gadgets and gimmickry: Dodge join the fight to win back customers in 1932, during the Depression. At least the family is still believable. (Chrysler Historical Collection)

SUPÉRIEURES PAR LA SOUPLESSE DE
LEUR MOTEUR INDÉRÉGLABLE SANS SOU-
PAPES-SURBAISSÉES DONC PLUS STABLES
D'UNE SILHOUETTE PLUS SÉDUISANTE
SPACIEUSES-SEULES MUNIES DE 4 VITES-
-SES SILENCIEUSES : 6 CS - 6 DS - 8 DS

PANHARD
PARIS

be in business twelve months later. Hupmobile, for instance, took pains to explain in their advertisements that they owed no money, owned their own plant, had no mortgages and debentures and intended to stay in business. So they did, but several times they were forced to suspend production, and finally gave up the unequal struggle in 1941.

Of the popular producers, Clyno was the largest casualty in Britain, and R. H. Collier, who purchased the spares and goodwill, spent much time and money entreating public and trade *not* to treat the Clyno as an 'orphan' make. Some large American firms were also in trouble; Durant failed in 1932, taking with them 'sister' makes Locomobile, Star, Rugby and others. Willys-Overland and Studebaker both survived periods of receivership, and Reo gave up to concentrate on trucks. In Europe, Cottin-Desgouttes and de Dion Bouton were typical of the pioneer makes which succumbed. In the luxury market the proportion of failures was highest; many driving into bankruptcy to the purr of eight cylinder-in-line, the final folly of the 'Twenties.

But if the outlook was grim, it was not reflected in the automobile advertisement of the early 'Thirties. New art forms were making their appearance under the influence of Adolphe Mouron Cassandre, and added to the escapism of the 'Twenties a surrealist fantasia, in which all the women

Opposite: sans soupapes: Kow follows fashion with this stylized Panhard in 1931. (National Motor Museum)

Confidence triumphant: the mountain road theme, with the car driven far too fast and with its wheels too close to the unprotected edge of the precipice recurs constantly. Here Curmo extols the virtues of *traction avant* to a Spanish audience.

appeared to have been drawn by Lapage. Later the boyish figure and the semi-shingle were finally replaced by the Jean Harlow image of womanhood with its long-lashed feminine line.

Travel, exotic foreign places and, following the awakening of interest in all things Egyptian after the discovery of Tutenkhamun's tomb in 1922, a strong middle-eastern influence (page 107) could be seen with pyramids and the Sphinx as favorite backgrounds for travel scenes.

A period of violent experiment in art styles led the avant guarde, in the persons of Ashley Havinden, E. McKnight Kaufer, Cassandre and others to fight traditionalists like Sir Frank Brangwyn RA. Brash new typefaces ousted Stephenson Blake, and there was a return to the wretched clutter of the First World War era when photographs were positioned uncomfortably alongside artwork with a bewildering shambles of different typefaces (below). Some advertisements looked as if the copywriter, whose appropriation for the year had been halved, was nevertheless determined to cram the same amount of words into the purchased space.

Very little had been seen of a directly sexually evocative nature in motor advertising with the exception of early classical or mythological references, and females were still depicted as either eager young slips of things in summer dresses wielding tennis racquets and Kodak Brownies, smart women about town with fox furs adrape, or elegant theatre-goers in full evening dress. Fiat provoked the wrath of the Vatican itself when they employed all the veiled

Voice in the wilderness: with a mixture of photography, artwork and sundry typefaces and sizes, Dodge's preoccupation with cramming the last selling point into the last square inch is typical of the worst of 1930's advertising. They were by no means alone, however. (Chrysler Corporation)

VOL. 16, No. 1   JANUARY, 1939   FOURPENCE

THE *Ford* TIMES

Double entendre – unintentional: if ever there was a more damning indictment of the machine age then this must have run a close second. Doubtless it was not Weeks' intention to portray an individual apparently on the point of nervous breakdown, but that is the impression given.

Lukewarm Luton: Vauxhall not trying very hard in 1931.

Competition: reflecting Mussolini's colonial interests
is this North African flavored scene which appeared
in 1939. Alfa Romeo was Italy's prestige car during
the 'Thirties, having passed into State ownership in
1933.

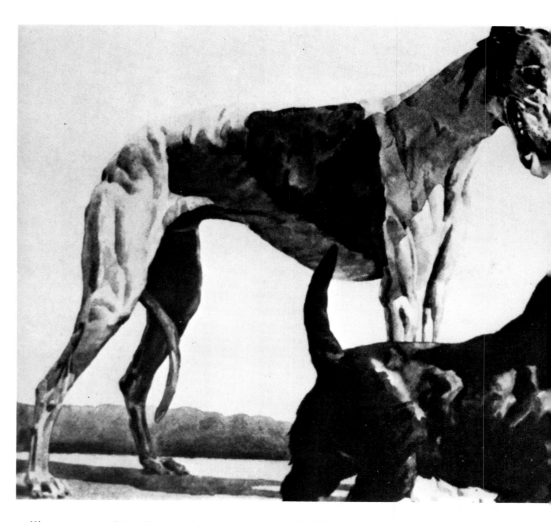

pulling power of the female form to plug the Balilla (page 120). An edict was duly issued insisting that the lady's skirt be draped more modestly, concealing the too-inflaming curve of her left buttock! Fiat complied. It was, however, to be many years before anything much more daring than a swim suit would be used to promote the motor car.

A natural hangover from the 'open road' fad of the 'Twenties – and the desire for open and sports-type cars it had engendered – was the 'soft' sports car. Beloved of the 'Promenade Percy' from the Riviera to the Pacific Coast, and good fodder for sea-side *concours d'elegance*, it encompassed British products like the Wolseley Hornet, Singer le Mans, Hillman Aerominx, Triumph Super Seven, and anything open, rumble-seated, and preferably brightly colored in America.

Both the German and Italian motor industries received massive state support in subsidies for export, and in motor racing and development programmes. As a result, probably more European cars found their way to Britain than ever before. Size, however, diminished the appeal of the larger American cars despite their attractive price, and the continuation of the horsepower tax in Britain proved a severe deterrent. Everywhere a note of economy was to be found – even among the glamor products – and the cars which sold best were the small ones.

If the 'Twenties had established the small car, the 'Thirties consolidated its position, and even in America babies like the American Austin were able, with the help of imaginative and sometimes sensational advertising, to last the decade. It was the era of the Topolino, the Austin Seven and the Morris Eight, and the importance nowadays attached to Pierce-Arrow Bentley, Duesenberg and similar models as being evocative of the age is more the product of nostalgia than anything else.

Each country chose its own path to recovery. In America it was Roosevelt's 'New Deal'; in Italy, Mussolini; and in Germany, Hitler. And with Hitler came

No use, Mac, it's a FORD V·8

Better than most: the humorous restraint, composition and execution of this American Ford offering for 1936 shows what could be done, Depression or no Depression. (Ford archives, Dearborn, Michigan)

the Volkswagen, perhaps the greatest aid to Germany's *post-war* recovery – half a generation after the demise of 'that man'. But the 'strength through joy' car and the efforts of the Nazis to promote it in the Fatherland, provided a foretaste of what was to come. For the first time motor car advertisements incorporated nationalist propaganda. When the inevitable conflict occurred, the efforts and talents of copywriters and artists alike became the stone upon which the axes of politicians and militarists were ground. Not that their services to motoring were missed. Very few private cars were offered for sale in Europe after 1939, and in 1942, following Pearl Harbor, the cessation of private car production in America removed the need for widespread advertising. The immediate post-war years, beset as they were with material shortages, needed none of the competition and imagination of pre-war advertisers to boost the sales graph, and such lip service as was paid to the art was for many years either merely a reminder that motor manufacturers were still in business or bald statements of fact about the product.

The World of Rolls-Royce

In a time in which excellence is no guarantee of commercial success, the sustained position of esteem enjoyed by the Rolls-Royce motor car is unique. Whilst it is true that the marque did not grow from humble beginnings in the accepted sense – Royce was a successful manufacturer of electric cranes, and Rolls a wealthy aristocrat – the earliest advertising of the company gave little hint of the restraint which was to characterize its later pronouncements. This 1906 example is typical:

> Any car can *crawl*
> up a hill,
> fitted with a low gear of 6 to 8 miles per hour.
> Remember that the
> Remarkable
> Records of the 20 hp
> Rolls-
> Royce in
> Rushing up the steepest
> Roof-like gradients kindly selected by
> Readers of *The Motor* are made with a gear-
> Ratio which at 1,000
> Revolutions of the motor per minute gives
> 15 miles per hour on the lowest gear and
> 50 miles per hour on the highest gear.

Nero fiddles whilst Rome burns: there are some who might find this scene of the idle rich at Ascot, and the liveried chauffeur opening the Fortnum's hamper, a little incongruous in the year which heralded the Wall Street Crash and the Depression. 1929.

ROLLS-ROYCE
THE BEST CAR IN THE WORLD

ROLLS-ROYCE LTD., 14/15 CONDUIT STREET, LONDON, W.1.

138

This preoccupation with speed appears incongruous from a company who, over the years, have consistently refused to comment on the power of their engines except to confirm that they are 'adequate'. It was, however, the introduction of the Silver Ghost – with all that the name implied – in 1906, and the withdrawal from competition from that year onward, that signalled the change in policy which was to ensure lasting success.

In terms of mechanical innovation, the Rolls-Royce was not remarkable, and the Lanchester, for instance, of the same period employed more advanced features. Royce was, however, single-minded in his insistence upon attention to detail, and even detractors had to admit that the Rolls-Royce was beautifully made. It was probably the decision to adopt a one-model policy which ensured the consolidation of the luxury image, and since the Ghost had demonstrated so effectively its qualities in an RAC-observed 15,000 mile trial of 1907, the decision to concentrate upon its refinement for the following eighteen years had a profound influence upon advertising policy.

The point was that the Rolls-Royce customer knew exactly what he was getting without being told. There was no year-by-year face-lift to 'date' last year's model – just steady, often unannounced, improvements throughout the car year by year – and if last year's owner recommended the car to his friends they could be sure that the car they ordered would incorporate all the refinements which had endeared it to him. It is this unchanging standard of excellence, which could always be relied upon, which made the extolling of the car's virtues in advertisement copy entirely superfluous, and the coining of the phrase 'The Best Car in the World' the only slogan necessary to capture the imagination.

Rolls-Royce became a living legend. Governments fell, frontiers changed, but a Rolls was always a Rolls, and what had originally been a trade name became synonymous with quality. When George Brough built his motor cycles to his own ideals of perfection, they were advertised (with Rolls-Royce's blessing) as 'The Rolls-Royce of motor cycles', and everyone knew what was meant. They still do.

In many ways there are parallels to be drawn between Royce and Ford: the single-mindedness, the concentration upon and refinement of, a single model over almost two decades, the restrained tones of the advertising material, the reliance upon the product to advertise itself.

This similarity is also at the root of the folklore which grew up around the Rolls-Royce. Whilst people told jokes about the Ford, they wove sagas about the Rolls, and whilst the factory never associated themselves with any of these, the effect was to elevate the car in terms of world-wide esteem to a position in which it must have been hardly necessary to advertise at all.

There were, of course, those who attempted to topple them from this perch. Hispano-Suiza at one stage produced an advertisement identical in layout and restraint to that of the Rolls – with the slogan omitted – but if this caused consternation in the Rolls camp it was not obvious, and it is possible that potential Hispano buyers were discouraged by such a vulgar lack of taste.

The habit of depicting the Rolls-Royce against a regal background was also widely copied, but whilst this may have carried a little weight with firms like Armstrong-Siddeley, no one was seriously impressed when the same tactics were employed to boost sales of the friction drive G.W.K. and other 'plebeian' types. The American Roamer, which belonged to the select band with Rolls-type radiators, attempted to carry the illusion further by enlarging the first and last 'R' in the name, but Rolls-Royce treated this with the contempt it deserved, and the only firm to be honored by an action for infringement was Sizaire-Berwick.

The First War brought with it a fresh crop of legends surrounding both Rolls-Royce aero-engines and armored cars (favored by Lawrence of Arabia, who also bought seven Brough Superior motor cycles), and when, in 1922, Rolls-Royce felt obliged to cater for the burgeoning middle classes with their stolid 20/25, the Ghost was continued for a further three years to 'preserve' the

Opposite: stately homes mandatory: wrought iron gates, coat of arms and pillared portico may not have looked out of place for Rolls-Royce. The theme was, literally, 'gate-crashed', however, by everyone from G.W.K. to Austin Seven, and the results in those cases were little short of ludicrous. *Circa* 1933.

Brand imagery: it is all here, stark yet subtle; the Grecian porch echoing the radiator shape, the evening dress and liveried flunky, and the silence as the party glide off to the opera. 1934.

image. Its replacement, the Phantom series, was destined to remain in production, in modified form, until 1939. The image of unchanging quality was maintained throughout the period, and the only serious mistake Rolls-Royce ever made was to open a separate factory in Springfield, Massachusetts.

Whilst the American Rolls was an excellent car, it suffered from one overwhelming handicap – it was built in America. Not only did this throw it into direct competition with makes like Peerless, Pierce-Arrow, Cadillac and Packard, but it destroyed the charisma (so far as American buyers were concerned) of the legendary British factory presided over personally by the arch-priest Royce himself. Those who wanted the best continued to import the British-built cars, and the Springfield factory closed in 1931, at the height of the Depression.

Apart from this lapse, Rolls-Royce management – like Henry Ford – never failed to understand the psychology of their customers, and this is still demonstrated both in their advertising and manufacturing policies today, which is probably the main reason why, when the Packard, Hispano-Suiza, Delaunay-Belleville, and Isotta-Fraschini are now but memories, a Rolls-Royce is still a Rolls-Royce.

ROLLS-ROYCE

AS SILENT AS ITS SHADOW

ROLLS-ROYCE
The Best Car in the World

ROLLS-ROYCE LTD. 14-15 CONDUIT ST., LONDON, W.I. MAYFAIR 6201

Acknowledgements

The author and publisher would like to thank the following organizations and individuals for their help in supplying information and photographs for this book.

Adler
Automobile Association
Bosch
British Leyland
Burberry's, London
Carless Capel & Leonard Limited
Castrol
Chrysler Corporation
Daimler Benz
Dunhill, London
Dunlop
Fiat
Firestone
Ford UK & USA
Gamages
General Motors
Jaguar
Lancia
Lucas
Michelin
National Motor Museum
Opel
Peugeot
Pirelli
Renault
Rolls-Royce
Royal Automobile Club
Society of Automotive Historians
Society of Motor Manufacturers and Traders
Shell-Mex & BP Limited
The Veteran Car Club of Great Britain
Michael Worthington-Williams for his considerable assistance
and co-operation in producing the editorial content of the book.

Index

143